T0031554

THE
FUTURE
of
SONGWRITING

THE
FUTURE
of
SONGWRITING

Kristin Hersh

MELVILLE HOUSE UK
LONDON

THE FUTURE of SONGWRITING

First published in 2024 by
Melville House UK
Suite 2000
16/18 Woodford Road
London E7 0HA

and

Melville House Publishing
46 John Street
Brooklyn, NY 112001

mhpbooks.com @melvillehouse

Albert Einstein quote from *The Ultimate Quotable Einstein* collected by Alice Calaprice
(Princeton University Press, 2010), originally from an interview with G. S. Viereck,
"What Life Means to Me", *Saturday Evening Post*, October 26, 1929.
Reproduced with permission from Princeton University Press.

Jacques Attali quote from *Noise: The Political Economy of Music* trans. Brian
Massumi (University of Minnesota Press, 1985). English translation copyright 1985 by
the University of Minnesota. First published in *Bruits: essai sur l'économie politique
de la musique*. Copyright 1977 by Presses Universitaires de France.
Reproduced with permission from University of Minnesota Press.

A CIP catalogue record for this book is available from the British Library

ISBN: 978-1-68589-117-6

3 5 7 9 10 8 6 4 2

Printed in Denmark by Nørhaven, Viborg
Typesetting by Roland Codd

If I were not a physicist, I would probably be a musician. I often think in music . . . I see my life in terms of music.

ALBERT EINSTEIN

Fetishized as a commodity, music is illustrative of the evolution of our entire society: deritualize a social form, specialize its practice, sell it as a spectacle, generalize its consumption, see to it that it is stockpiled until it loses its meaning . . . but at the same time, it heralds the emergence of a formidable subversion.

JACQUES ATTALI

I'm glad to be alive.

SISTER ROSETTA THARPE

Introduction

My father pushed me over the fence at Woodstock when I was three, into my mother's waiting arms on the other side. Then he climbed over himself and joined us for a few days of music and face painting. I don't remember much of this, but I do know that it wasn't my first concert. And we lived on a commune, so our lives were mostly music and face painting anyway. The songs that informed my childhood were a Southern hippie mashup of rock and Appalachian folk songs; one top-down, the other grassroots. Each had their moments. And since I don't want to be rigid, I allow for a sweet spot in the corporate world, when art and entertainment meet up and promotional money backs something truly musical; something more giving than egotistical.

It's my feeling that this is the exception to the rule, though. When I started my first band, Throwing Muses, ten years after Woodstock, I had studied classical guitar for years, and had written close to a hundred songs. The sonic vocabulary I developed was in no way marketable. It *might* have been art, but no one would call it entertainment. And it definitely sounded like a mashup of rock and mountain music, but without wearing those influences on my sleeve, I'm gonna say it sounded pretty nuts. Songs themselves had completely filled my world. They were my gods: uncontrollable, otherworldly and running the show.

Invention is like that. It doesn't strut or pose; it's raw and often kind of uncomfortable. On the shoulders of giants is how we grease that grinding wheel we just reinvented, slipping our soundtrack into the ears and lives of others. Songs are sound bodies and when we respect them, they tell us how to love them. As someone who never wanted to be a pop star, I was always very clear on not wanting to be a part of the problem. The problem of using promotional money to buy success, of sexism, of marketing to an imaginary lowest common denominator. It took me a long time to extricate myself from the world of corporate rock and forge a grassroots DIY path on my own. There was no real template to follow except to bring the past into the future: to begin again as a songwriter in the faceless tradition where songs themselves shine, rather than the people who play them.

In this book, I liken songs to medicine and musical response to laughter, because I'd like to engage both songwriters and listeners in an attempt to dig a tunnel out of the dark days of corporate interest and back to the raw timelessness of collective invention. The book highlights some interesting multidisciplinary conversations I've had to that effect – 'the comedian' represents these – with luck they're hopeful and not too grim. I do believe the human heart and its desire for song can weather this storm of fashion economy we've been living for about a century, and find its way back to true songwriting: to the raw, to invention, to both visionary and collective. To an artistic and sociocultural self-correction; toward living song bodies and away from dead product.

Heat

It was still hot, though the sun had gone down a while ago. Hiding behind my tent in a metal folding chair had become my habit after the show: every night, sitting in the dark with my bare feet in the grass, listening to the strange soft clicking of eucalyptus leaves in the branches above, trying not to hear the murmuring voices of people leaving my show below those branches.

I almost threw up.

What a strange woman.

Bats in the trees.

As our audiences filed out the front, a comedian buddy playing the festival in the tent next to mine joined me, dragging over his own metal chair. He said nothing. We watched the stars.

Christmas in Sydney is a hot thing. Makes you study hot things around you all over again, because it's freakin' *Christmas*, so they seem more striking. Hot things like sun on metal and shining glass. My apartment building on Sydney Harbor was distorted by both of these that summer, in that year of two summers. Gold sunlight bent by metal-framed sheets of glass up so very high: a man-made sheen. And it only shone, did not reveal, as glass is supposed to; looked like a black and white photograph. I would stand on the sidewalk outside my building, looking up, counting, trying to find my floor and understand how it is for humans on earth, all crammed together and sweetly lonely, building things. I carry the next song like a new baby everywhere I go, so each of these images relates to my new musical creature —and its future. Will this new song be happy, be healthy? Can it shine without lying? I write it sweetly lonely, building something. But really, it writes itself and it's not lonely, just alive. And its sheen is out of my hands.

I left *It's a Wonderful Life* playing on the TV in my flat pretty much round the clock; a comforting dream America in strong juxtaposition to my homesickness. The movie framed it so cartoonishly: shone, did not reveal, as homesickness is supposed to. Man-made in black and white. I don't know what Australian television station decided that broadcasting one movie 24/7 was "programming"—seemed more like a glitch—but I was grateful. Like keeping a town in your house that you could visit whenever you felt overwhelmed. *It's a Wonderful Life* wasn't *helping* my homesickness, exactly, just adding nostalgia and narrowing its parameters: forty-something Christmases piled up behind my eyes and through the eyes of my children. A crammed together and sweetly lonely thing.

The sidewalk outside my building burned; Aussie kids down near the ground so close to its burning. Happy children, usually with ice cream, but still. Seemed at the mercy of a frightening element: heeeeeeeeat. They were very much like the bats in the trees overhead, with an immediacy and beauty in movement that makes lying impossible. Little truth-homunculi, sweaty Christmas beasts down low by the shop windows.

▶ ▶ ▶ ▶ ▶ ▶

"Is it nice or sad that they spray fake snow on stuff?" I ask the comedian beside me. "I mean, does the heat make them defensive? Wistful? And what's it made out of?"

I'm actually groping for a sense of our future, which is what we always do when we're together. Reaching, maybe, but I continue to hope. Hope that I live songs as he lives laughter, and that we both will continue to *live*. I've learned that a true song doesn't belong in the entertainment industry any more than a bat belongs in a skyscraper, but entertainment's the only game in town. And laughter? Seems to bridge that gap, so I rely on my comedian in a feedback loop of hope and hopelessness.

We have established that neither of us wants to be famous; fame is associated with a lack of quality in our experience, and with a truncated career path. If you're "in" you're gonna be "out" next year, by definition. We want to *work*, work in the corner, work forever, and we define "work" as a substantive endeavor leading the way, rather than the coming on to the crowd that star machines and marketing teams bore us with. That old story: vanity vs. soul. So in this particular poker game, we lay down the Jack of Diamonds—in Tarot, the messenger—and we study it. He carries messages between this plane and others; materialistic yet spiritual. Arts and entertainment, inspiration and work, vision and marketplace, for goddamn ever. My comedian buddy and I like the card we draw and its enthusiasm, but we are fully aware that fear waits in the wings, and in our weakest moments, will incite vanity, which leaves us lost in the pile of cards, of people. Jack of Diamonds. It's in the deck; the deck that seems stacked against us, against substance, against small, against healthy, against giving.

My career trajectory was one of signing on to corporate patronage only to jump ship in horror at the sexist product they demanded. There was no music in that equation, and no humanity, either. Just a kind of sad whoring of commercial jingles. Commercial music is a *commercial*, and it is hardly ever music. I didn't know corporate was a pimp. It took a goddamn long time to extricate myself from that beast and begin to parse the elements of egoic reward vs. visceral truth-telling. *The fashion/status game may be the only game in town, but that doesn't mean we gotta play it* is how I view my story.

My comedian calls it *how the fuck are we gonna eat?*

Anyway, here's where I was goin' with sun sheen, man-made gloss and steaming children so low to the ground: fake snow as a truism, an opportunity to bridge that gap, like the laughter my comedian inspires with his work. Art *plus* entertainment, substance plus style, and maybe they could get *along*, of all things. But don't goddamn sell, you know? No selling, no stars, no status, just pass the hat so you can work again. And maybe that's not real snow decorating your hat, but it draws the listener in with its prettiness, and in that, it's an outreach. Be like a child, in other words: close to the ground, observing, forgiving, beautifying, uglifying, adventuring: play.

My friend kicks off his shoes. Too hot for socks, so he also shoves bare feet into the midnight grass. Doesn't wanna talk about fake *anything*. Why would you? Such a beautiful night; those stars and cool bats calling for the real, for hope and substance and depth. "The show, the show, the show," he sing-songs. "Where'd we leave off?"

All month we've been engaged in this shattering, goofy debate, our depth of concern masked: we laugh, then wince. We are very, very worried about our future and the future of our two passions. His for laughter, mine for songs, the monetization of which has been consigned to corporate industries. Not sweet fake snow, but bullying greed. How the hell do you get along with *that*? We're having trouble figuring out how to bring art and commerce together. So we begin by trying to figure out what it is we do, or try to do, given that we're both on sorta shaky ground at this festival. Shows are hard for shy people.

"Well," I answer, "I had submitted to you that jokes and songs were expressions of the same impulse. Capturing an inspired moment and rolling it into a little clay ball we then roll to others, so that they can enjoy it," I tell him. "We loved our response to the initial inspiration so much that we want to engender it in *them*."

He raises his index finger at me. "I had submitted to *you* that this is true only of *good* songs and *good* jokes."

"Right. Forgot." I'm kinda bored. So tired of the quality conundrum. "The lousy kind are opportunistic manipulations of that response, right?" He nods, listening vaguely. "A bad song *isn't* a song. It's sound, like fast food is calories, but it's not sharing, it's selfish . . . with an eye toward money and attention." The bats are active at this time of night, getting ready to fly; their squeaks and rustling blend with the murmuring of people. I dearly love the bats. I'm sure I love the people, too, but they scare me sometimes. "Attention being the currency, the commodity and the problem."

He turns to me. "Would you like to submit that?"

"I submit to you," I nod, eyebrows high, "that work without inspiration is *not* work, but merely facsimile."

"Fakers," he grumbles. "But people *laugh* at bad jokes, you know. And they *like* bad songs."

I chuckle. For some reason, under the midnight bats, I find this funny, not sad, though it's both. "Yeah, they're starving in a parking lot, trying to live off fast food. But there's an apple tree around back behind a dumpster. The tree doesn't advertise, so, unfamiliar with apples, people don't realize it has food growing on it. Nobody's making money in that equation. Nature and human nature are the same, but it's hard to champion apples when so many people don't know what they are."

"Real songs and real jokes are real food?"

I think. "We call this a culture when really it's just an economy. And our chief export is entertainment."

"Chief," he repeats, smirking. "Wanna submit that?"

I sigh, watching the bat-flutter above. "Nah, I'm good."

"When was the last time they recognized an apple as food?"

I splay my hands, incredulous. "I guess right before we tried to take credit for apples. To own songs and jokes. To sell them, attribute them to our-*selves* instead of our selfless moments. Publishing and ownership and bought spotlights as an artificial marker of attention to quality. And bigger money than passing the hat, so the middleman—the business itself—profits." An entire tree empties itself of flying foxes, who form a cloud over us. "Oh my goodness, how fucking cool," I breathe.

He grins mightily and lifts his palms to the sky. "Thank you, Australia!" The bat cloud breaks up into smaller bat clouds which, shattering and shrill, disperse into even smaller ones.

"Thank you, Australia," I sigh. "People all over the place recognize apples as food. Industries don't recognize *them* as *people* because they aren't the buying public, corralled for their money meat."

"Money meat," he nods. People are still filing out of tents. Because we've chosen to honor our shyness above our selling, we still have some hiding to do if we don't wanna run into audience members. My friend leans back happily, hands behind his head. "Tell me again about the blue octopus," he says quietly, gazing up into the deep dark.

The Blue Octopus

Aaaah, now the blue octopus is fun. Much better. I lean back in my chair and speak to the stars. "The blue-ringed octopus," I announce, "is approximately four inches in diameter—"

"Four inches high?" he interrupts.

I think. "Wide?"

He considers this. "*Heighth!*" his tongue sticking out. "Breadth. *Widths.*"

"I like 'diameter' cuz an octopus is squishy and should be able to shape itself however it wants," I say, defensive. "Which is what I submitted to you only last *night*, remember? Cuz metaphor. It can change its shape and turn upside down without us trying to goddamn *measure* it. Like we try to goddamn do to *everything*."

He shakes his head. "Okay, calm down. No need for cursing. Then liken it to an object of similar size."

"Good one," I tell him. The canvas wall of the tent behind us whaps in a hot breeze. "The blue-ringed octopus," I begin again, "is roughly the size and shape of a baseball. It is highly venomous and can be dangerous to—"

"No it's not."

I look at him. "Of course it is, that's the whole point."

He blinks. "It's not a baseball. It's not *like* a baseball."

"Oh. Well it is *sometimes*."

His patient voice. "Your conviction that it can do or be whatever it wants—"

"It's squishy!" I announce happily.

"—that it's *squishy*," he continues. Then stops. Natural sounds take over, the murmuring of people dying off. An orchestra of singing insects.

I wait. "What?"

"Nothing."

"They don't even *play* baseball here," I point out sheepishly.

"Squishy yet unmalleable. Just go with that, I liked it. Fluid yet responding to internal cues and a core sensibility, not market rewards." He folds his arms and closes his eyes, ready to listen.

"Market rewards?" I screw up my face. "The blue octopus?" I was *really* ready to leave the Jack of Diamonds lying in the deck.

Smiling, his eyes still shut. "Take external validation off the table."

Studying him in the dark. "Are we making this about *you* again?"

He opens one eye. "Of course!" Then closes it again, settling in.

I shrug. "Alright, buddy. You can be squishy. And unmeasured. You may take any shape you want. And you're oh-so-dangerous, cowboy." The heat does actually dissipate at this time of night. A bit. Lower temperatures work their way into the city as the wind picks up. "The blue-ringed octopus is eleven centimeters in *size*—"

"Ooooh, metric system, nice touch."

"Quiet. This marine animal, this cephalopod—" He snickers, eyes still shut. "*Quiet*. Is dangerous to humans, its venom containing a powerful neurotoxin which shuts down the heart muscle and causes paralysis as well as respiratory failure." My friend shudders happily. "Its *painless bite!*" I continue and he smiles. "Often goes unnoticed by the victim."

"Unnoticed!" he cries, gleeful.

"By the *victim*. Think about it, you'd fling that little guy across the rocks if you knew what he'd done to you."

"If you knew you were his *victim*," he agrees.

"Evolutionary mutation is miraculous." We love this little creature cuz it's an unnoticed performer, imagine that. The work shining, not the person. Just a carrier of venom-medicine, looking for a vessel. How could you trust any other equation? This octopus kills people, so maybe beware, but he has a definite effect and he does *not* show off. As a songwriter, I have to believe that in the future, we will celebrate songwriters who disappear; songwriters who transcend self-expression and self; songwriters who evade the spotlight by turning it on the listener, even when no one is listening.

Not sure my comedian shares this hope, so I don't voice anything too hippie-happy tonight. I can hear them breaking down the PA system inside my tent now that the audience has wandered off. Laughter and banging around, my sound dude's voice. "So: are we the blue octopus, and the venom the work, and the audience the victim?"

"Mmmmm . . . comedians are that mean. But you aren't. You're nice. The song is the octopus and you are its victim. You share the venom that has ruined you with your last breath. Anybody who comes across you all full of poison is your audience."

Jesus, I feel sick. "That's very pretty," I grimace. "Thank you."

A look of consternation shifts the comedian's features, though he keeps his eyes shut. "Here's a thing: they laugh more at your shows than mine."

"Well . . . you gotta set up your jokes. I surprise them. They don't expect to laugh, so they do."

Opening his eyes, he looks dubious. "They call me strange," I tell him. "I'm not strange. I've just had some weird things happen to me." Our audiences are taking a long time to skedaddle. "Substance doesn't have to be strange. 'Pop' just means popular; doesn't have to be dumb, *shouldn't* be dumb. Any human is capable of depth, just by virtue of being alive."

I once released a record with 50 Foot Wave called *Free Music* that didn't cost anything. Hoping to, you know, "free" music from the almighty dollar, from the imaginary concept of a lowest common denominator, as an experiment. Two million downloads in, The Industry came knocking, freaking out: *who are you, we need catalogue numbers, we have to count your sales, you aren't allowed to work in secret, you must apply for money measurement*, etc. When I explained to them that this record didn't *make* any money, they hung up, sighing in relief, and never bothered me again. This experience was illustrative for me. I never forgot the bureaucratic panic; the counting, the measuring, the impression of listeners as consumers, not participants.

"So jokes and songs," I continue, "are material reflections of an energetic singularity: inspiration. Just a split second of Big Bang burst and we take a picture, carry that Polaroid along a linear time-line and you know, show up holding it. In a tent in Australia at hot Christmas time." He watches me try to build on this, squinting. "Not to impress anyone; you're just carrying the Polaroid, hoping it'll help somebody, saying, *this exists now.* The show? Isn't showing *off* then, it's showing *up*." He considers this, moving his lips while he repeats the sentence silently.

The Jack of Diamonds rolls his eyes.

"We are purveyors of venom," my dude intones, unblinking, as a tall man wearing rabbit ears, a body suit and platform sandals appears around the corner of the tent and stands in front of us. We look at him.

"*What* did you say?" the rabbit asks.

"He said that we're purveyors of venom," I tell him.

My comic nods. "Squishy crustaceans."

"They're not crustaceans, dumbass," shaking my head. "They're cephalopods."

"I know," he grumbles, "I'm just drunk." The rabbit shifts his weight, looking from one of us to the other, an elaborate smirk on his face. He is also playing this festival all month and often checks in around midnight, after his show ends, as his audience is leaving. They sound happy, drowning out the insects with their own buzzing.

"We were, uh . . . discussing humility in the work-place," I explain. "Show as showing up instead of showing off." The rabbit stares. "We were discussing our future."

"Tell him," whines my friend to me. "He isn't safe."

I look up at the rabbit man. He's wearing heavy pancake makeup. In this heat. "The blue-ringed octo-pus has enough venom to kill twenty-five humans in a few minutes."

The big rabbit raises his plucked brows. "Okay . . ."

My comedian buddy frowns. "How could that even happen?"

"I don't know." I think. "Twenty-five people at the same time? Tidepooling?"

Rabbit Man makes a *yikes* face, sighing happily. "So how'd your shows go?"

"I think a guy actually threw up tonight," I tell him.

His *yikes* face gets *yikes*ier. "Really? Like, inside the tent?"

"No, he left. That's how come I'm not sure if he puked or not." I look up at him, sad, but he's not really listening. I truly wish my work didn't upset anyone.

"My show was *wild*!" he squeals and is about to tell us just how wild when my friend groans.

"Dudes! We haven't done the best part!" He gestures toward me grandly. "My lady? Please continue."

The rabbit, wind swept from his sails, looks insulted. I try to remember where I left off. "Uh . . . squishy and unmalleable—"

"No!" My friend throws his arms up in enthusiastic frustration. "The! Blue! Octopus! Isn't . . ." he leads me.

"Oh! Sorry, yes! The blue octopus isn't . . ." Catching the rabbit's eye. "BLUE!" Jazz hands.

The comic claps. "Until?"

We're boring the big rabbit, who hobbles away from us on his platform sandals in the grass, shaking his bunny ears. "Until!" I yell and then drop my voice so the rabbit has to come back and peek his head around the corner of the tent to hear me. "He . . . kills . . . you." I stage whisper at him. Two fists in the air from the comedian. "We're thinking we gotta not shine, not call attention to ourselves, sneak up on the audience and slaughter them when they least expect it. Not about us and our shiny blueness; it's about the venom and who might need it."

The rabbit winces. "No wonder they throw up." He takes his leave, hobbling around the corner of the tent.

"Don't go tidepooling!" I call after him.

"Okaaaaaay!" he calls back.

The bats in the trees. Hundreds of silhouettes. An Australian moon and Australian stars. We admire the sky and the insect orchestra and the eucalyptus branches, emptied of their flying foxes, gently clicking again; the spectre of the tiny blue murderer who isn't blue until he's a murderer.

This is all lovely, but as usual, we have solved no dilemmas. The Jack of Diamonds remains poker faced on our drunken debate table, and all we can do is face him again, both of us afraid of losing this game. My hope that the past may hold the key to a future of egoless songs is a tough sell when the entertainment industry determines our creative weather conditions, but I don't see any other way forward than: the bad guys fall down. Which, in this case, means: the part of us that wants to be *big* is discouraged, making room in turn for a lovely smallness. And the resulting songs? Could reflect a small world/big picture orientation both idiosyncratic and universal. We need this *now*, so I'll try to see it in the hands of future songwriters. Children now, I guess. Children who see clearly, and hell, that's what children do best.

The comedian turns to me sadly. "I wish *I* could make people throw up."

᛫ ᛫ ᛫ ᛫ ᛫ ᛫

We haven't seen each other's shows at this festival, out of respect for our friendship and the experiential division of our unique disciplines, so as we walk back through the park, we're careful to address only issues of engagement, not quality or drive. Quality is so precious, drive so suspect. This forever-long debate is only to ask ourselves: 1. Why do we do this? and 2. Can we keep doing it?

The first question comes with happy baggage. The sensuous engagement of a body with a mind in it: small world, big picture. Spinning self-conscious-ness into self-awareness, as an awakening that rears its head in a series of little Big Bangs. Your senses turned on, body in charge without falling to hedon-ism, it shoots a person straight to heaven, feet on the ground, in the mud, even. Laughing, crying, peace and music sit there together; the only spell we know that will bring about Life.

Next comes the enthusiasm of sharing it. Childlike, we figure, in its humility and fun. Fun isn't stupid in a child's hands, but an animal orientation; an unself-conscious, natural state. Which'd be not so much an awakening as a remembering: you were born knowing this stuff cuz what else is there to know? Born living this stuff, cuz what else is there to live? And the feminine principle, in its earthy, dark and physical embrace of what is unknowable, with a healthy dose of yang light. We love talking about *that* stuff. *That's* e-e-e-e-easy.

The second question is tougher, its baggage uglier, because whether you're discussing an individual psychology or a corporation, once "sharing" is viewed as an opportunity to attract attention and make money, the shared product is subject to facsimile, imitation, the weakness of a presentation that prefers style over substance, self over others, is no longer timeless, but merely fashion. When one doesn't respect one's audience as people but manipulates them as consumers. They are reduced to what's in their wallet, in other words. The big, fat dumbing down for a lowest common denominator that doesn't actually exist. People are unique and complex. They only appear otherwise when you sell them *that* notion, along with the dumbed-down product.

Eventually there is no work left at all; just a performer in a spotlight, pretending, showing off. Flirting without heart, the performer will never love you, is only dressed up as a lover hoping to fool you into engaging for a moment and paying for it. A zombie apocalypse of sorts, on both sides. This is the weakness the business of music—of all entertainment—succumbs to when it denatures human nature.

The people gone, we walk slowly through the park to our flats by the harbor. My friend weaves a bit, so I aim my guitar case at his knees to subtly urge him back onto the path. "Music should be *low*," I grumble. "Not snooty. Should be in everyone's hands."

"That's their excuse for making it dumb," he mutters.

"Jesus, yeah." Lampposts lining the path glow hazily. "It's *not* music. It's a play cast with actors dressed up in costumes that match a sound-style. A *song* would have to be . . . life, a body, right? Reality is raw and dangerous and sweet and embarrassing and heart-on-the-line, skin-in-the-game."

He shakes his head. "That's uncomfortable. Marketing'll sell 'em a script they're familiar with cuz real life is unpredictable and scary." Wincing, I look up at him with my saddest *help* face. "Right?" he winces back.

"Yeah. And boring sometimes."

"So the goal in the entertainment industry . . ." he starts and then stumbles onto the grass. "Is fooling the easily fooled."

Shooting at his smarts with my index finger gun. A beat. "And making it about a person instead of the work. What their name is and celebrating their resource hoarding and shit. *Are you bigness? Do you have a big name? Did you make big money? Did you make lower humans build you a mansion? A pyramid? Was a sound you made on a chart? Are a buncha people watching you? Did you step on heads to make people look?*"

"Jack o' Diamonds," he says quietly, finding his footing on the path again.

My guitar case bumps on the ground when I slouch in defeat, which I seem to do whenever the conversation brings us back to the Jack of Diamonds. Materialism and spirituality misapprehended when they have been, could be, the *same energetic.* Our two obsessions will never let us view real work as pointless, but the frustration of lifting your head from that work and seeing the maelstrom of shallow making so much noise, coming between work and audiences, between lovers and loved, blocking eyes and ears from their own simplicity and depth. So I straighten up and hold my guitar higher, reminding myself that the bullshit can't possibly win. "The bullshit can't possibly win," I try, and he half-smiles down at me.

Music and laughter happen all over this planet; all over this life thing. Inspired moments are usually uncelebrated because we don't ask them to pay our rent. Why celebrate what is already a celebration? The fan/star relationship, however, like any sycophant/royalty relationship, is an unbalanced one of want; unbalanced in its resource hoarding and constraint. Inherent in its success is growth and expansion. Those hungry ghosts cannot get enough on either side because there is no love between them, and without love, there is no work. Instead, the performer and audience are engaged in something symptomatic of a sociocultural disease: the cancer of status. Of course, this particular cancer can pay its rent, while my comedian's Big Bangs he calls jokes, and the bewitching, quirky children I call my songs, can't always. Cancerous cells don't know or care that they're bringing about the fall of the system; they're concerned only with proliferation. "Success" and "failure" are reversed in this equation. Success of the individual is failure of the system.

Twenty years ago, when I became listener-supported, it was with a heavy humility that I assumed was how begging felt. Which: yeah. But

without any real *humiliation*, the financial equation
I was trying to pull off—studio costs covered in
exchange for free music—really just felt like a
company picnic. A buncha goofballs who know how
goofy they are, hangin' out, balancing soggy paper
plates in somebody's back yard. There was no longer
any pretense of pro, of gloss, of marketing or status;
of anything but musician and listener engaged with
song together. No success, no failure. Circumventing
the industry, an individual at odds with the universal is off the table. The individual *is* the universal.
No one can be bigger or smaller, higher or lower,
than another when there is no attention-seeking, no
hoarding of resources.

Musical success begins and ends with the compos-
ition: the song breathes, it lives, and a few people are
gonna live back by making it a part of themselves.

Go Limp

On stage, my friend uses his life to trigger laughter. Sounds so light, is so dark. I am currently using mine to trigger tears, though that wasn't my intention. A stage show based on my first book, it's a teenage diary set to music. Songs about songs, essentially. Sounds so light, is so dark. And yeah, it makes people cry. And vomit, for Christ's sake. I feel pretty bad about this, so the rest of the show—roughly eighty percent of its content—is funny. As a kind of apology: a worried smile and a punch in the arm for the audience.

When I tell the scripted story of how I began hearing songs, I stand in front of projected images a friend painted and I play guitar. Noodling, I guess, because to me, everything that happens comes with an inherent soundtrack. I'm also telling the audience how to feel with these chords and melodies, which is a cheap trick at best, and probably the bullshit manipulation I accuse others of. I kinda don't care because it's how things happen to me, *at* me—with a soundtrack—so I'm not lying. Just pressuring them to adopt another's sensory experience for a couple hours.

To be fair, this show wasn't *my* idea. I would sit in an alley with my face pressed into my guitar, slowly starving to death, if everybody left me alone. But some people have a positivity that translates into this idea that you hawk the snake oil *even if it's medicine*. It's just what ya do, cuz maybe it could help somebody. You carry that Polaroid to hot Christmas. And I like music very much, so I say yes when they use me as a proxy for their positivity. I get on the plane, in the van, on the stage, and I say yes and I become invisible. I accept the syringe of memory that is a song, and if it's embarrassing, I try not to be embarrassed; if it's funny, I try not to laugh; if it's sad, I try not to cry; if it's angry, I try not to be pissed off.

Straddling your essential self and the selflessness asked of you as a vehicle for a song is tricky and messy, since songs demand full sensory engagement. We like to associate our senses with ourselves, but that's sort of missing the point. You're a body, you're a life; if wind is the blowing and rain is the falling, then living *happens*. Will plus fingerprint equals a you, and you-ness is reflected in a song: self minus self. Tricky, like I said, but I don't believe any song without this equation is real, is music. Luckily, songs adore messiness.

The images in the paintings that move slowly behind me while I play are urban elements in natural landscapes and natural elements in urban ones: birds in cities, garbage in meadows. I imagine this works because people—in our attempt to be civilized animals—often seem ill-suited to one environment or the other. As if we keep trying to breathe under-water or swim in the air. But these paintings are so thickly effective that it helps you feel okay about being naked here, tumbled from Eden and climb-ing back. We are all thickly effective in our layers of stories.

This painter painted to my music. When I learned that, I decided that I didn't want to see her paint-ings, but when confronted with them, I found that they were places to go. We became friends in that moment, and I used these landscapes behind me to help apologize for the strange stories I told. She would often tell me, "Don't be scared, I got your back. I know you're shy, I know about your stage fright, I know. But I am my work and my work is behind you. I'm right behind you." She died too young, but leaving behind places to go is like making little planets before your atoms shoot apart. Entire worlds. I was stunned when her paintings didn't die with her, in other words. They continued to help me tell strange stories; something I did in case it could help some kid who needed them. Help prepare them for the things that happen here.

One thing that happened here is a slow-motion car accident that cracked my skull in three places. I flew up into the air and stayed there, at least in my experience of it. Stayed up there floating over the street long enough to hear a voice telling me that I was about to hit my head harder than I'd ever hit it before, so: *go limp*. As soon as I let the stuffing of my own will fly out—the will that keeps our atoms from shooting apart—the cement flew up into my face and smeared off my features. Turning over, I saw that half of my left leg was gone, no foot at the end of it anymore; the sky over my jagged shin bones a brilliant blue. I was between child and adult then. Where I remain today, like most people.

This kind of crashing thing happens to people all the time; we're fragile, life is violent, we break, we work with broken, we heal. Not a tricky metaphor to carry wherever you need it, wherever you'd like it to go; so I told this story in my Australian festival tent. And maybe the man who stumbled off the bleachers and eased himself through the tent flaps to vomit had lived this and did not want to relive it, wasn't prepared. Or maybe he had *never* lived a violent breaking and didn't know it could happen; wasn't ready, wasn't prepared. I'm not sure which of these orientations makes you throw up. I do know that usually when we're upset, it is one or the other: *I wasn't ready for this to come back* or *I had no idea shit like this ever happened.* Both of these imply a *please just leave me out of it* that life was never gonna do for us. If you are alive, you don't get left out of life. You can *miss* it, miss your senses all turned on, miss your story's tactile nature showing itself through your skin, your eyes, your proprioception, your listening nature, your body's everythingness and freakin' ESP, your lusts and lightness, the layered memories of your own psyche. You *can* actually miss all of that. But you don't want to. And life still happens at you when you try, anyway. Might as well have some skin in the game. Skin is what makes music and music's body is a song. If everyone who called themselves a songwriter rode these thermals? The ones people living life laugh and vomit through, cry and hold each other up through? We'd all be lighter for it.

I only talk about blood and shin bones in this show—while noodling on my guitar like a stoner roommate—because the event that cracked open my skull also cracked open my songwriting. Until that day, I had imitated other songwriters, had played to impress, to make something cool. It was a dead process; not recycling, just garbage again. Which is without invention. After I floated and fell, though, my sonic vocabulary formed itself into its own planet that had very little to do with me, was a place to go. I *heard* the music now, because I went limp. We must go limp, can't fight life; life is everything.

To me, this is songwriting. Music making its own body through yours.

⊦ ⊬ ⊳ ▸ ▶ ▶

"I don't like the show," the comedian says to the trees around us in the midnight-blue park.

I turn to him, my guitar case bumping against my knee. "You don't like your show?"

"I don't like *The Show*. The big rabbit likes The Show."

I think about this. Our footsteps on the path are the only sound within the insect orchestra, its crooning buzzing drowning out traffic noise. "I don't like The Show, either; they *make* me do it."

He looks shocked. "Who makes you?"

"The positive people, you know. Don't you have positive people?"

"Like managers? Yeah, but . . ." he twists up his mouth. "I thought you were driven."

"I'm driven to write the next song and make it sound like itself. But managers, agents, record companies, publicists, they all think, *this is good, let's share!*" I make a worried face up at him because this confuses me, always has. "*You* know."

"Sharing is nice," he admits. "But they want us to show off, right? And then money."

I sigh. We're back to this again: the Jack of Diamonds. "And then money. Which isn't wrong. Right? That's what the positive people tell me, anyway. Cuz, you know, starving to death isn't good for sharing, isn't good for work." I swing my guitar case like I swung my lunchbox waiting for the school bus when I was a kid. Except it's bigger than a lunchbox, so it throws off my center of gravity and hits my comedian in the leg, kinda hard.

He stops for a minute to rub his knee and glare at me. "*Big* money is wrong," he decides. "People always suffer when big money happens."

The sound of our footsteps amid the insect buzz, which is still drowning out traffic. I trust insects more than cars. "Yeah. But you gotta stop saying that. This is why people hate us. Capitalism is a lottery ticket they grip very tightly." Our conversation is slow because it's late and we're tired from our shows, but we're even *more* tired of this problem. "Royalty and Hollywood royalty and political royalty and rock star royalty and corporate royalty all think God gave 'em their money," I grumble. "And everybody else keeps 'em there by paying attention and voting with dollars, believing the emperor's new clothes. It's all they know, and you can't argue them out of it because it's all they know, and it's been this way forever. They aren't *gods*, we're all *God*, all of us little pieces of responsibility. Tasked with being *un*selfish."

He looks down at me, eyes bugging. "*You* gotta stop saying *that*."

"Well, I know, this is my point. I don't say it out loud, exactly, I just say it to *you*. You don't count." I punch him in the arm and he punches me back gently, sighing. "It's okay, buddy," I tell him. "We like the work itself. When everything you've seen pulls itself into this little beast in front of you and bubbles out into a life form. Nuthin' fancy, just a little seed in a paper cup. You sprinkle water on it and push it into the sun. We love that, we *live* for that."

"I remember those little cups of seeds. Sunflowers?" He looks both enthusiastic and bleak. Possibly because of our shared homesickness and nostalgia, but tonight, it seems like little seeds really could be everything. "My mother, my kindergarten teacher, my Scout master. *Everybody* gave us paper cups and dirt and seeds. God, what was up with the little seed thing? That was the best. Life in dirt."

"Real life is in the dirt, and that's the goddamn truth." I look straight up, the stars in the dark little seeds in big dirt. "All us little kids holding tiny life in dirt. That was what we needed to know." Briefly reflecting on the seventies and a childhood without seatbelts or rules. "But yeah, it was a cheap way to entertain kids, I guess. Dirt, little paper cup and a sunflower seed. How much could that have cost?" More headlights, running across the path now. We're getting closer to traffic, closer to people, closer to shining apartment buildings. Gotta leave the insects' and flying foxes' world soon, so we slow our steps, keeping pace with the swaying trees. "So how do we ... become the big rabbit and *like* the show?"

"Well, we haven't seen his show." He shrugs. "We may not want to be like him. If he's cool, we could get some pointers."

"You're saying and not saying that it's the insubstantial work that shows off?" I ask him. "You always say that."

Flinching. "I don't want to be rude. I just think the substantial is a square peg at the show."

"It's not the substance's fault and it's not the show's fault. It's money behind what the spotlight shines on, hoping to get more money. We're used to an entertainment industry that counts on the audience being shallow enough to wanna look at shiny." More headlights, fewer trees, fewer bats in those trees. We're getting closer to civilization and farther from animals. "So most people who perform, even without promotional money behind them, jump right into showing off and skip the actual *work* part of working."

"*And they're right!*" he whines.

"Noooooo, nobody is shallow. By definition! At essence, you can't be superficial."

Shoving his hands in his pockets angrily. "*You* always say *that*."

He's right; I do always say that. It doesn't help to believe that people are good, but I like it. "How might one . . ." I wonder out loud. "How might one hold up a paper cup full of tiny sunflowerness so the good folks could see it?"

"Therein, my girl," he sighs. He really does seem drunk now. *How's he getting drunker?* "How do we give them what they don't want?"

"What they don't want *yet* . . . what they don't want *anymore*. Before spotlights and star machines and marketing and royal patronage, was a physicality of expression that spoke more clearly in this way."

"When?"

I try to imagine an era we should have lived in, but I can't really come up with one that didn't celebrate shallow. "Well, not measured by history, but in every life as it begins."

"I hear ya. Ambition means you wanna stand in the spotlight and make everybody look at you," he slurs. "But if your work is real, shouldn't you be . . . I dunno, *working?*"

Such wild brightness just beyond the trees. Headlights are not un-beautiful. "If I think that I'm trying to impress anyone or imitate anything . . . you know, wondering, *will this play well?* The work stops breathing: it *dies*." He nods, considering this. "So I put down the guitar until I'm a cooler person."

"But I *want* to show off," he whines. "So that nobody thinks I'm a failure."

"You just don't want to be a failure. Which you can't be because your work is valid."

"And if nobody sees it fall in the forest?" he says to the trees around us.

"If all that's listened to is lousy songs, I'm not gonna play lousy songs. I'll maybe hold up my paper cup on a street corner so people can see my sunflower." Grinning up at him. "And I'm wondering *now* if the wild craziness humans inject isn't beautiful sometimes. There are sunflowers everywhere, but if you grow one in a paper cup and hold it up for people to see? The fake and the real together could highlight each other; could be a little . . . stunning."

His blank face. "What if they don't look?"

Shrugging. "Still a sunflower." I smile up at him. "I don't like being looked at anyway."

Some headlights run across the leaves and trunks of the acacias around us. *Here come the people*, I think. I think this a lot. "Whaddaya wanna do tomorrow?"

"It *is* tomorrow."

We're standing on a sidewalk now, waiting for the stoplight to change so we can cross the street where my building is glistening, bright as the lights reflecting off of it. Sydney Harbor is on the other side, in the distance. It glistens, too. Man-made has a distinctive wildness for sure. Whatever future songwriting has rests in this balance. The insect buzz and the skyscraper sheen. Eye candy, ear candy, candy, fashion and flash used to better themselves; recycled trash. Could we offer substantive shimmer? Could you play what sounds like glistening Sydney Harbor? Play shining flying foxes? "Some cool things shine," I tell him, but without any segues, I've lost him and he has no response.

"Whaddaya wanna do *today?*" he sighs. "Museum?"

The light changes and we cross the street together. "Museum. Who taught you *that* word?"

He shrugs. "It's got art in it, apparently. Thought you liked art."

"That mean naked ladies?" I fuss around in my bag, looking for my key card.

My comedian looks tilted. I study him, wonder if I should walk *him* home; something I never do. Maybe I *am* a bad lady. At least a bad friend. He clears his throat. "I think art is naked ladies, yes."

"Cuz men," I say, holding my key card up and studying him. "Y'all aren't actually in charge you know."

"Yes, ma'am."

"We create life."

He squints. "Sorry, ma'am."

"Y'all are probly *afraid* of us."

He nods and tilts more. "I am absolutely terrified of you." He looks seasick.

I watch him fall against my building. "You okay?"

He stares for way too many seconds. "I'm good!" he shouts suddenly, spin-swaying off the wall, using drunk momentum to push his floppiness into something like walking away.

"Don't go tidepooling!" I call after him as he rounds the corner toward the harbor.

"Okaaaay!" he yells in a fair impression of the rabbit man.

ꞮꞮ ꞮꞮ ꞮꞮ ꞮꞮ ꞮꞮ ꞮꞮ

Songs didn't always have writers. There was a time when the body of a concise piece of music with lyrical content was an influence affecting and effected by the many voices which participated in it. Not always together, as the word *chorus* implies, but over time. A song could be walked from town to town, carried over the ocean, taught to children who shared it with their friends and later with their own children. A "piece" of music: music is ongoing—a river racing past—we just grab a *piece* of it sometimes, if we're lucky. We don't create real music, we listen; each of us a unique sculptor with a set of fingerprints unlike any others. Pressed into the clay of a song, we leave a mark because we lived, but we didn't invent clay. We merely alter it. If we're honest, it is a raw and beautiful imprint that we leave. If we misinterpret this symbiosis as self-expression and convince ourselves that we're bigger than the clay, selling ourselves instead of sharing the work, we leave an impression of our greatest weakness: attachment to the impression we make. There is no work in that equation because there's no love in that equation.

That particular weakness grabs and distorts the concept of a *chorus*. It moves us away from falling in love with a song and making it part of our deepest heart. Moves us away from the selfless giving that is its own musical reward, as our most shallow of hearts is inflamed by a new fashion. The idea of music making more money than passing the hat is fairly new. A hundred or so years of an industry taking credit for songs—for fish caught in the music river—and selling copies, attracts those who hunger after the easiest of earthly rewards: diminishing people. In your eyes and in their own: "You want this," isn't music. "I'm bigger than you," isn't love. A true song is like a true heart: timeless.

But marketing is mistaken; there isn't a sucker born every minute. No sucker has ever been born. Suckers are made. All of us are unique, and that isn't encouraged because it doesn't make us reliable shoppers. But the weaponized selling that tells us experts know what we want is crumbling. We won't have to wait long for a distinctively un-capitalistic future to redefine selfhood, and who else cares enough to jumpstart your heart when you hear a song? It will not be the shopper an ad said you were. The future is filled with beating hearts that race when a song speaks one of their truths.

It's a long elevator ride to the seventh floor. I have plenty of time to think.

Pick Your Own Apple

Jimmy Stewart is telling Donna Reed he's gonna lasso the moon when I finally get my key card to work and the heavy door vacuum-seals shut behind me. The couple is not yet a couple this early in *It's a Wonderful Life*, but they're throwing rocks at a house about it. A house that no plastic key would get them into. No plastic, imagine that. He's also telling her he wants to build skyscrapers, though, so he's headed in the plastic direction. At least in the shining metal and sheets of glass direction, where I sit in this apartment, uniquely removed from bats and sunflowers, and from Donna Reed's music and children and home. Which is the point of the movie, I guess. He learns nature through human nature. As in *Tristan and Iseult*, a woman is the carrier of this biological and psychological information.

Donna Reed throws her rock at the house. They're making wishes and her wish is not skyscrapers. The bathrobe she's wearing is too big for her, dragging on her pitching arm, but her rock sails into the window anyway, shattering the glass, because her wish is an inspired, fundamental one. Ill-suited to her outfit, fighting against irksome time and space, the aim of yin is still true. We're on *her* side, but the glint in Jimmy Stewart's eyes looks like hope, looks like hunger and adventure, and we love those things. The feminine may carry the kind of nature that shows we've lost our way, but the masculine carries its own cool. Some action is right action. All of this in everyone, just occasionally underrepresented or misapprehended.

Stepping into the shower, I hear them singing "Buffalo Gals" together.

I've probably seen this movie like, fifty times in the last week, though never once through. Looks like a timeless story played out in time, like a lot of cool things. Like people. Still not sure where time and timelessness come together. In our unique fingerprints, I imagine. Each of us as special as everyone else and no less special for that.

The question of the denigrated feminine is more troubling. That we don't sense the female energetic as nature, aesthetics, instinct, creation, quiet, body, darkness, receptivity, is culturally myopic. These qualities are in everything and everyone and in true love and true work. If industry and its marketing distort the feminine as a shallow, unbalanced thing, we lose a cultural impression of the cyclic qualities we need to balance our masculine arrow of growth we call 'success.'

We lose the child in this unbalancing as well. Children are not silly; they are life. And they aren't less intelligent than adults. They carry different qualities which inform their knowledge, and we have a lot to learn from them. A body that feels and a mind that follows is an orientation unique to young humans. We should grow *toward* that, not away from it.

An alive song reflects nature's rawness just like a kid embodies it. The fashion sound that is for sale out there? Does not.

There is a small window above my head, with five stars and half a moon showing. Shower spray blurs the image, as I blink at it, trying to see clearly. Same moon Jimmy Stewart wanted to lasso.

Everyone is born with a visceral response to music; the ability to recognize an apple growing on a tree. We lose this connection, this ability to feed ourselves, when marketing tells us what food is: it's packaged, it's for sale, it's industrial. It has no personal relationship to you, to your nature, as it has been *de*-natured. The land apple trees grew on? Is "owned" now, the trees gone; songs and food come from buildings now and it all costs and makes money. Those *aren't* songs, of course, any more than fast food is apples. They make sounds, like fast food has calories, but Nature is not selling, so she looks gone, and we don't remember a time when she grew apples for us.

We are all also born with the ability to *write* a song, to pick our own apple. We lose this concept when corporations tell us that expert culture runs this sphere like any other; that only those dressed up as musicians, attracting attention and making money ("professional" means making money) have the ability to write our soundtrack. When in fact, the opposite is true: no one distracted by egoic rewards like money and fame is in the state of raw selfless-ness that attracts a song. Even more so now that the public's attention is merely bought with promo-tional money.

Blinking through shower spray at the moon.

"I don't like the show." My poor drunk comedian buddy's plummet from enthusiasm for laughter to distaste for the spotlight. Where does it go wrong?

Too many years of people showing off on stages, I guess. The moment of inspiration, though: the first breath of a song like the intake of breath before you laugh, a syringe of memory that will become your next thrill. That would be the work, right? We craft as best we can in response to that Big Bang. Music grows a song body this way. *Listen*, we say. *Maybe this'll help.*

My favorite future: that a venue would just facilitate the listening process. Musicians would push their little cups of sunflower into a spotlight to help people. To "show" them a little piece of the will that keeps our atoms from flying apart: *and look how damn nice it is.* Not pretty, just beautiful. Sometimes ugly, but still beautiful, because what is beautiful is what is necessary. Which is often body-low or spirit-high, but always what is most necessary: water in the desert. That'd be culture. *Pop* culture is an economy's pseudo-culture; an opportunistic take on grassroots and zeitgeist that makes big companies big money.

 ⠀⠀⠀⠀⠀ ▸ ▸ ▸ ▸ ▸ ▸

Suddenly, I realize I'm still just staring at the moon over shower tiles, water dripping down my face. *Should prob'ly do something else.* Pulling my towel up around me, I drag an ottoman close to the TV

as the neighbor dude in Bedford Falls throws down
his paper in disgust because Jimmy Stewart won't
"kiss the girl." Sydney Harbor shimmers behind me.
Dripping on my ottoman, I figure I'm close to getting it: tied up in resources and status, The Show
joins hands with an economy of competition that
music itself has no patience for, so it's not there.
The chorus, the ancient and fundamental group
effort toward song, could help a piece of music
last hundreds of years. If someone takes credit for
it, though, sells copies, inflates their own image
as bigger than the song, it may last an inflammatory moment. That encourages a lack of depth, a
lack of engagement: *y'all are so dumb, you'll buy
this*. A true song isn't dumb, so the industry rarely
sells true songs to true listeners, they sell product
to fans: 'radio songs,' essentially commercial jingles.
Commercial 'music' isn't music; it's a commercial.
Marketing as the product. Fashion by definition.

For a song to last a hundred years serves no one
if, to you, attention and money are the rewards;
if you fear that your body will lack resources and
the impression you make will be low status. If you
have never actually heard a real song, seen an apple
growing on a tree. Which is not uncommon now.
Fashion-sound is an industry, and as such, subject to

competition. The cooperative that was once a song? Has left the room.

My comic's sadness. *"I don't like The Show."*

Could you shine a spotlight on that first breath of inspiration worked with honest fingerprints into something shareable? Or are spotlights only bought for show-offs? Show-offs don't show off what's raw about themselves; they do the opposite, smoothing their edges, trying to appear better than life instead of presenting as carriers of life. A misapprehension of selfhood as something selfish. Given this, it's pretty amazing that so many gorgeous moments of song have slipped into our culture from all directions— even corporate marketing—cuz none of us want to stop our collective heart beating. How lovely.

I glance behind me at the moon over Sydney Harbor. Through dark glass, it looks dim, diminished. Jimmy Stewart asks Donna Reed what she wished for, but she's afraid it won't come true if she tells him. Truth is fragile in the light. You tell somebody the truth and they wonder what you're selling. We're rightfully suspicious, living in a marketplace. What's selling *now*? Tomorrow's garbage.

But garbage is not un-beautiful.

Wandering over to the black glass adjacent to the kitchen, overlooking the water, I wonder about planned obsolescence, about making all this garbage on purpose. About asking music to play the marketing game. If you freeze a body in time, you're looking into zombie eyes. No true song would ever let itself walk dead; all love wears aliveness on its sleeve. Maybe patience with the zombie eyes until they move forward and catch up? Until they move back and remember?

I'm sure I have my own version of zombie eyes, but I haven't heard songs differently, moving through time. I'm vague on their origin—the fuckin' sky or magic or something—but still, all I have to do is listen whenever I feel like disappearing into that void. And when that void lets you go, sometimes you're carrying a piece of clay. Sometimes that piece of clay is better for wearing its impression of your little loser fingerprints. Sometimes not. I don't publish songs that aren't for sharing. Nothing to do with quality, just keeping my kids inside on a rainy day. And then there are the rainy days we all race out into, thirsty for a waterfall; you never know. Gotta listen to the songs, can't tell them what to do.

⏵ ⏵ ⏵ ⏵ ⏵ ⏵

Jimmy Stewart and Donna Reed are again called out by their neighbor for Not Kissing. He throws his paper down in disgust, slamming his screen door shut behind him. I have a pipe-smoking neighbor, too—at home in New Orleans—but he doesn't read the paper when he's on his front porch, he plays saxophone. Puts down his pipe to make squeaky coolness. "I never liked saxophone until I heard you play it," I told him once, and this was true. I needed somebody to kick it out of gloss for me, I guess. This man doesn't play glossy, so it prob'ly wouldn't matter *what* instrument he played. Same with the drummer in her garage around the block who doesn't play tasty, doesn't follow rules. And the kid in his basement with a buzzing amp who plays so simply and lyrically: enthusiasm. The lady two blocks away who plays a trumpet in her shed—reedy, wistful melodies, when I'd thought trumpets were fun. And the babysitter who plays slow harmonica at nap time. He's the only one of us who plays for others because he plays for those babies, but none of us would say we play for *ourselves*, exactly. It's just the fingerprint us humans press into sound waves. More and less than a bird call because our species is so complex that we get fucked up easily, lose touch with both instinct and aesthetics. Dendritic neural pathways, roots and branches, their directions so explicitly undetermined. Nature lets go of us when we let go of nature. That mother doesn't always keep us in from the rain, but she'll join us under a waterfall. The less comfort we seek and the more exhilaration we feel, the closer we get to our branches reaching in the right direction, and balancing. We are Nature's fucked up children and she doesn't love us any less for it. In tumbling from Eden, we're tasked with building the raw muscles of simplicity in an over-complication of our own chaos. Can't leave instinct or aesthetics out of any equation. Plastic keys won't get us into that house, in other words. But songs will. And music is everywhere. It'd just be unusual to find any in the music business. Not impossible, just unusual.

Art Bones

The stylish museum docent has to ask my friend to step away from the painting a few times. "I didn't touch it!" he announces happily each time she reprimands him, like that's an accomplishment. Hungover, he's red-eyed and fuzzy, but also springy and lighter than he was last night.

I make a *quit it* face at him. "Dude, what're you doing?" I whisper.

"I wanna smell the paint." Like this is obvious.

"You're *smelling* the paintings?"

He laughs. "Not the paintings, the paint. I wanna smell what the painter smelled when he was working."

I squint at him. *What a freak.* "He *or* she."

"Geez, give it a rest, Gloria Steinem. Read the plaque." He leans in to another painting and the docent looks up, frowning, from her little chair in the corner.

Now I kinda wanna smell the paint, too. Leaning in to the painting with him, I whisper, "That's *Ms. Steinem* to you, buddy. And some women are named Michael." The painting just smells like the room as far as I can tell. It smells quiet. It smells dry. It smells echoey. "*Can* you smell the paint? Just smells like museum to me."

He breathes elaborately, inches from the canvas. "Maybe museums smell like paint."

The docent sits up straighter. She is dressed like Art. Like a grown-up. Her outfit suggests that we don't get it. So does my friend's behavior, though. "Then quit it and just breathe in fumes. You're stressing the lady out." Instantly over it, he races out of the room, nodding to the woman as he leaves. Hurrying to catch up, I smile at her and she smiles back with angry eyes. I forgot that I wanted to tell him about Jimmy Stewart and Donna Reed. Seems important in a building of trapped art.

I find him in a room where bright orange tubes are sticking up out of the floor. "Did you see the sign?" I ask him. "DON'T SNIFF THE TUBES."

He's folding his arms and staring down into one. "I saw it." The tubes are alone in their own room. Kinda space-agey and cold.

"So I was watching *It's a Wonderful Life* last night and I had some questions."

"Yeah?" He stands, arms akimbo, admiring the tubes.

"Yeah." I try briefly to appreciate the tubes also. "I figure it's okay if Jimmy Stewart *wants* to lasso the moon, cuz then he hears Donna Reed's stone land at the end of the movie and land *hard*, right? So we could be cool with corporate power because it lays the groundwork for a substantive . . . you know . . . *revolution.*"

Suddenly, he's over me *and* the tube exhibit and racing out the door. *Shouldna said "revolution."* Rolling my eyes, I follow, talking to his back. "Okay, not revolution, just *change*. If the Jack of Diamonds grew a sunflower, he'd just be facilitating a process. Let's bring that back, that's all. The superpower of invisibility. Don't give to receive, right?"

He nods vaguely, then stops short to peer into a room with cool melted sculptures in it.

"The messenger between," I continue. "Anybody could do this, everybody *should* do this." Rejecting the sculpture room, he walks on, saying nothing. "Talk to me." But he's too busy being fuzzy and racing around. "And then we *show* people our sunflowers," I babble, "that'd be the show, no stars. Just cuz maybe they'd be happy or less lonely—"

"Or they'd throw up," he says, checking out a wall lined with black and white photographs.

Shaking my head. "You're just jealous cuz I can make people puke and you can't." I poke him in the chest. "So we *show* people. That'd be the *show*. Get it?"

"Jesus, yes." The photograph wall does not pique his interest enough to warrant being still.

"The show wouldn't have to be shallow or make us shy then," I insist. "Before it was a business, there might have been some quality associated with attention." We're both wearing ratty old sneakers, so our footsteps make no noise; unlike the other museum patrons whose shoes click loudly down the hallways and between the Arts. The sound of grown-ups, like the angry docent.

"I like that," he agrees. "We wouldn't have to play goddamn dress up or pretend to be a hosting a fuck-ing *party*, all smiles and shit."

I shake my head, disgusted. "Dude, no need for cussing. You don't gotta work blue; you're better than that."

"Sorry, ma'am. Wanna see the rocks and sticks room?"

"It's okay. I know you're tortured or whatever." Looking up at him, I see how *beleaguered* he is. Poor guy. "Rocks and sticks are okay, I guess. I wanna see the bone room in the brochure."

"They have bones? I thought that was the *other* museum. The dinosaur one."

I point at the wall of bones in the pamphlet I'm holding. "Art bones."

He squints down at it. "Oh, *art* bones." Suddenly racing away again, he almost runs into some museum patrons dressed incongruously in beach attire. Guess we didn't hear them coming because they're wearing flip-flops; quiet shoes, like ours. Blocking them, he opens his arms and grabs their shoulders. "Please forgive me." As they nod uncertainly, he pulls me away with him, jogging serpentine around the group.

"You sure are zippy today," I tell him, tripping. "You look like hell, though."

He stops suddenly. "Those weren't questions," he says, scouring the hallway.

"What?" I check the map in the brochure to see where the bone room is.

Something catches his eye. "Your *It's a Wonderful Life* questions weren't questions. And none of it had anything to do with *It's a Wonderful Life*."

"Oh yeah." Studying the map, I figure it must be upside down, but reversing it doesn't help. "Oh, it's sideways." I look up from my brochure and realize I've lost him again. He took off somewhere, I guess; found his rocks and sticks maybe.

Just to my right, I spot a café with a deck overlooking the water and decide that's where I wanna be. It looks sunny and breezy and empty, so I order a coffee to earn a table and join Australian air and seabirds. Sitting down to wonder at them, a shadow looms up around me, blocking the light. I turn around slowly and see the comedian, looking affronted. "What are you doing?" he demands.

I think. "That a trick question?"

He folds his arms. "What are you *doing?*"

"Running away from you, *duh-uh*."

"Why? I'm your only friend."

"You are *not* my only friend and cuz you ran away from *me*." I turn back to my coffee. "Also, I think I don't get Art."

Dragging a chair away from the table, he sits across from me and folds his hands as if we're at a summit. "I'm your only friend in *Australia*—"

"You are *not* my only friend in Australia," I interrupt.

He glares at me, "—who gets it."

I stare. "Okay," sighing. "Tell me the *It's a Wonderful Life* answers, please—"

"Those weren't *questions*. And I'm familiar with your hippie rhetoric."

"Right. Sorry. Something about lassoing the moon. Yin and yang." I take a deep breath of sea air.

"Isn't this pretty! We are so lucky to be here." He waits, hands still folded. "So maybe it was the moon out my shower window, not the movie, but Donna Reed was throwing rocks and . . . I figure we're denigrating the feminine culturally, which leaves mystery, love, aesthetics and nature out of music."

"Okay, one: don't say 'love,' it freaks people out."

I nod and pretend to write this down on an invisible notepad. Then, gripping my coffee cup, I use it to point at him. "I submit to you that writing songs is a spontaneous, universal endeavor and a heavy player in our psychological makeup." He stares, silent. "And that placing the *facsimile* of songs in the hands of money, status and attention has left us with a twisted impression of spirituality and art."

He nods. "I thought you didn't *get* art."

"Yeah, well. That's prob'ly why." A seabird swoops by, squawking, and I shoot him my best surprise face.

"May I ask you a question?" he says. "How did breaking your leg make you write songs?"

"Oh. Well, I didn't just break my leg; I broke my skull and my face and my ribs."

He stares. "Okay, same question with more body parts."

"Because it didn't just break my body, it broke my self-concept," I say cheerfully. "Prob'ly all kindsa ways to do that. Breaking your *heart* is a good one. Or saving it. Having children so you learn that there's no 'you,' or at least that you aren't the story. Mine was being flung through the air. Important to learn early on that physics is not your bitch. And you know, we're mammals, but mammals attuned to time, to the finite, to physics, reflection, selfhood and empathy—"

Suddenly, he shoves his chair out from under him and jumps up to lean over the railing, his face in the salt-wet air cloud of Sydney Harbor. Leaving my cold coffee to join him, I notice that he's awfully rumpled, like he slept in his clothes. Poor dude doesn't have *It's a Wonderful Life* to keep him company, I guess. "Are you gonna puke?"

He thinks. "I'm pretty hungover," he nods.

"I'm sorry." The water is dazzling, shooting off crazy sun sparks. "Maybe don't do it at the art museum?"

Grimacing, he raises his head with effort. "Yeah, okay."

We stare across the water together, over the sun sparks. "Nothing changed when I broke," I tell him. "But when you see clearly that you're a body, sometimes you see clearly that you're a soul. You remember something you were born knowing." I strain my eyes across the harbor, looking for my apartment building, its gloss and flash. "Made my songs raw."

"Hippie," he giggles, rolling his eyes.

"Yeah, well, maybe hippies are right," I smirk. "Except people *like* hippies. They don't like raw; they think it's ugly cuz it doesn't afford them much comfort. Gloss and flash are the script they're comfortable with; equated with value because anything glossy is an ad for itself, you know?"

We squint across the water into nothing; a melancholy peace that we achieve occasionally, the Jack of Diamonds face up on our poker table. I often wish we could stay there, because comedy and songs are *in* the sadness and the peace: what do you do when faced with the ludicrous? Heliotropism, like a sunflower. You face the sun. You laugh, you play, and that's catching. He turns away from the water and looks down at me like it's time to change the subject, the activity, the day, the life.

"So . . ." I hum. "Wanna puke at the bone museum?"

⟩ ⟩ ⟩ ⟩ ⟩ ⟩

The bone museum has fewer bones and more children than we'd anticipated. Screams echo through the halls and toddlers chase each other in circles around us. I like this *way* better than bones, but my friend's hangover is more about looking for a dark, quiet, boring room. "Whatsa matter, don't you like thunder lizards?" I ask him.

He presses his index fingers into his temples. "Is that the noise I keep hearing? Thunder?"

I nod as we pace slowly through the running, screaming children. "That's thunderous applause for giant lizards that you're hearing: enthusiasm."

A little boy pushing a toy dinosaur in a tiny stroller uses it to chase his sister in circles and then runs into the back of my comedian's legs, causing his knees to buckle. The kids and I giggle shyly together as my friend raises his arms and shrieks at the children, T. Rex-style. They run away, delighted, and shrieking back at him. Walking on through the echoes of their screams, he yawns. "So those are the things," he says sleepily, "you keep telling me we should hold up as the gold standard of personhood?"

I think about this. "Yes?"

"Hmmmm . . ." One of the thunder lizards in the brochure catches his eye. I don't know why this particular one; they all kinda look alike to me. "Let's check out the Muttaburrasaurus."

I follow him. Which is easier now than in the art museum; marauding bands of children have slowed him down. The Muttaburrasaurus lives in a room that feels like a TV studio, and I flash on all the hours I've spent in actual TV studios, under glaring lights and waiting in green rooms to be *put* under glaring lights. The tiny audiences reading signs that tell them to clap, then stop clapping; people with headsets smiling blankly as invisible people in other rooms talk into their ears. The make-up rooms with clouds of powder in the air. I have never been able to shake the idea that what I do belongs nowhere near those places. "You do much TV?" I ask him.

He gazes into the dinosaur's jaws. "Enough to know it's weird."

"It *is* weird. So small compared to the range it has. And they tell you what to say. Did they tell *you* what to say?" The Muttaburrasaurus has a disconcerting dodo-esque head. "Why does this dinosaur have a film across his mouth?"

"I was just wondering that." He reaches out to touch the bat wings lining the Muttaburrasaurus's jaws.

"I don't love his eyes." We study its dodo face together as some children run into the room and then out again. "How come you aren't smelling the dinosaurs the way you smelled the paintings?"

"Uh . . . different process. I wanna participate in the artist's process. The bone guys, well. Not really sure what they do."

"Huh." We move around to the dude's tail. "Their job prob'ly smells like mud and then plaster. And then museum."

He nods, reading about it. "This one's named after a guy called Doug."

"Really? Muttaburrasaurus is named after Doug?"

"That's what it says here." Dinosaur calls—or what people imagine to be dinosaur calls—echo through the museum. As do the ongoing calls of children. "And yes, they do tell me what to say on TV. But they just tell me to say what I was gonna say, anyway."

"Yeah, I don't mean in, like, an *evil* way. Media training is real, though. Entertainment is a form and some jobs come with these parameters." We leave Doug the Dinosaur. "*That's* what I think is weird. 'Weird' meaning that I don't understand it."

"Well, no, you wouldn't, given that your qualification for work in the entertainment industry is that your leg came off once."

"This is true. And I never stopped wishing we could walk them through our —I'm gonna say 'process' cuz you're the only one here—our process. Smelling the paint."

"Yeah, don't say 'process' anymore."

"Hey, fossils!" I point in the direction of some trays filled with dirty, pointy teeth, hoping for something a little more sciency.

"Okay," he agrees. "Won't be any children in *there*."

We've slowed to plodding in our day. "Are you well-versed in the sphere of entertainment?" I ask him. "I mean, *comedy*. Geez. So positive. You might as well be a tap dancer."

He smirks down at me. "Yeah, comedians're all god-damn *vaudeville*, compared to you rock musicians."

Laughing, I punch him in the arm again, but today, this sort of knocks him over and I feel bad for witnessing this. He steadies himself as I frown in concern. "How much did you drink last night?"

"Enough." He rubs his bicep, shuffling into the fossil room. He was right; no kids in here. "I will say," he announces quietly, "that comedy is a litmus test of functionality."

My jaw drops. "Ooooh! I *like* that," I tell him. "Sounded really cool and echoey in this room, too." He peers down into some glass cases of dirty jaws.

"It's called *dying* when we fail up there," he says soberly. "If I can't pull laughter out of a room full of human beings, I die."

I'm totally caught off guard by this. "Jesus."

Nodding slowly, he adds, "I have as many different nuances for the word 'laughter' as Eskimos have for 'snow' and I'm at their mercy."

"I think I just welled up, buddy." We walk slowly, talk slowly. "I don't think I have a pass/fail measuring stick like that. Maybe if they dance." Kids race past, shooting each other with water guns shaped like dinosaur heads. "We should get some of those," I tell him.

He nods. "Yeah, okay."

"If songs and jokes are both sunflowers in paper cups, little pieces of . . . will. Of aliveness. Humble and high but not lowbrow or snooty—not bandwagon appeal or snob appeal—but making intelligent fun." He nods, holding a fossil up to the light. "If a song wants to be alive, then songwriters are here to facilitate that. But before I play it in public or release a recording of it, I have to step back and evaluate its *effect* or I won't know if it's *effective*. I have to pretend I'm a listener. It's my way of asking if they're gonna dance."

"No."

I squint at him. "No?"

"They're not gonna dance." We must have hit nap time or stimulation overload, cuz the crowds of kids are thinning out, the echoes of their cries less shrill.

"Oh. Yeah, I know they're not gonna dance. Anyway: how does a comedian pretend he's a listener when he already knows the punchline?" I point out the gift shop and a display of those dinosaur head water pistols and he lights up.

Walking into the shop, he picks up a plastic kite. "Is it windy today? We work in a park; we could totally fly kites behind the tents tonight after our shows. I bet the rabbit guy would join us."

"Oh, hell yeah, let's get three. Midnight kites! You have the best ideas."

He grabs three kites roughly and rolls them into a single tube. "I try jokes out on my friends. That's how I evaluate punchlines."

I look at him, blank. "I thought that's what *bad* comedians did."

"It is, but . . ." he lifts a water pistol up to the light and stares through its eye. "Bad comedians don't have funny friends."

I grab my own water pistol. "Think Rabbit Man wants one?"

"Of *course* he does." He shoots air into the air. "Tonight will be awesome."

Picking up another dinosaur gun, I grab four more to bring home to my children, then move toward the postcards. "So . . . is it that—and you know, as a shy person, this is hard for me to admit—we are a social species, so our output is partially determined by those for whom this gift is intended?" You can buy little fossils in this gift shop, as it turns out. We start playing with a shoebox-size display of trilobites.

"But if we *misapprehend* this equation and decide we're better or bigger or smarter than the audience, or that they are simply *marks* whose wallets we're after, we dumb down our product and joke's on us: music and laughter have left the room."

He twitches. "That . . . is . . . the problem." He runs his fingers through the fossils distractedly.

"It's also the solution?" I try. Glaring at me, he tosses a fistful of trilobites into the air, dropping a few on the floor. "Stop, buddy," I tell him. "Trilobites did nothing to you."

Sighing. "Why are you such a positive gal?" he demands.

I take the rolled-up kites from him. "Cuz what the hell else am I gonna be? It may not be about paying rent. Could be beside the point. Anywayzzzz: my *It's a Wonderful Life* question. Address it please."

"It's not a question," he mutters.

I carry water pistols, kites and postcards to the register. "Well, I can't solve these problems by myself." The smocked cashier has two gray braids and one brown tooth. I throw in four dinosaur pens and tell him I'm bringing them home to my children. The gray-braided man smiles at me over his smock, with his cool, mismatched teeth. "The pens are gifts for your children? Should I wrap them for you?"

"Oh wow, yes, please!" He pulls a long strip of dinosaur wrapping paper off a roll. Turning around, I see my friend in the hallway, steadying a child on the edge of a fountain. *Will ya look at that.* They are both tentative and balancing, and they both look gentle yet fearless; shy, yet open. Two children, just different sizes. The little boy slips and the big boy grips his arm, then they both giggle. "Better wrap one more dinosaur pen, please," I tell the cashier, and he smiles.

Never Forget That You Sometimes Suck

Walking to the show that evening, under the beautiful flying foxes who're just waking up, my friend carries my guitar case so I can juggle kites and water pistols. "That kid?" I offer shyly. "The one on the fountain?" And my friend winces mildly, like he's been exposed. "When I say everything comes down to kids, all I mean is *that*: guileless. And balancing. Be guileless and balancing and you'll know love and work."

Children aren't the future of songs and laughter just because we screwed up . . . they're literally the carriers of presence; of nature and human nature.

He smirks. "I know. Nice of you to give him a pen."

Huge, fluttering, leather-brown bat wings shuffle around in the leaves above us. "Good morning!" he calls up to them. "We all go to work at the same time; us and the bats and the big rabbit."

Smiling up at the sky beasts. "It's all upside down here in Australia: morning at night, summer in winter, little octopuses and big bats." Then I remember that we have a schedule to keep. "Oh yeah, we gotta give the rabbit his gun and his kite before his show. Do you know which trailer is his?"

"No, but I'm guessing it has a party in it." The sun is still baking this park, going down awfully slowly.

"You and that little boy were like two kids today," I tell him. "A *small* party. I think this is why you're good at what you do. Cuz you never grew up."

We walk slowly, though we're probably late for our soundchecks. Nice to see him not hungover or drunk. He still looks mildly beleaguered, but not bleary. "Every girlfriend who's ever broken up with me told me to grow up: *grow up or I'm breaking up with you*. And then she did."

"Oh." *Yikes.* "How many is that?"

He looks down at me, exasperated. "Well . . . *all* of them. They say we aren't good for each other and then they leave or kick me out, depending on how nice the apartment is." I think about this, but I don't like picturing him sad and bullied, so I stop thinking about it. "And then they say they wanna be *friends*.

Like I'm harmless." He gestures in the air with his dinosaur head water pistol.

"I'm sorry." Possible that a childlike orientation doesn't play well in the outside world.

He shrugs. "It's okay, I'm used to it." He aims his gun ahead of us down the path, peering through the sight over the dinosaur's open mouth.

We can see the tents now, and the trailers behind them. No audiences yet. This is the liminal part of the event: the circus going up. "You know, buddy?" I look up at him. "I submit to you—"

"What do you submit?"

"I submit that the child part of you was not quashed by an egoic belief in the hype of here." He squeezes the trigger and the dinosaur spews a stream of water. "Whoa! You put water in yours already? Cool!"

He studies the water dripping down his shooting hand, disappointed. "I thought it'd shoot farther."

"Just point blank, I guess." I watch as he wipes his hands on his jeans. "Personally, I'm looking forward to my children *not* being able to shoot very far with their water pistols." We're almost at the festival grounds. "They can draw quietly with some nice, dry pens."

Our soft footsteps, the leaf clatter, the swaying bats. "Your kids like pens?"

"Not particularly. But last time I came home from one of these festival stints, I brought them four kazoos," I frown, "and it . . . well, pens are better." He laughs. "I passed them out *as we were boarding a plane*."

"Wow!" he says, amazed. "What's wrong with you?"

I shake my head. "Incredible, huh?" The memory of four little boys' impression of musical power was so worth the noise and the angry passengers. Though the other passengers didn't *look* angry, I have to say. They looked really happy, pulled out of Grown-up Land for a moment. "It was instructive, to say the least."

He thinks. "How *long* did you let them play kazoos on an airplane?"

"Very good question. As I recall, about five years, but it was prob'ly less than a minute."

"Awwww . . ." He looks stricken. "You took their kazoos away?"

"Ha! You *are* a kid, see?" I grin. "Time is elastic. It was a very, very long minute. And, as I say, an instructive one."

Shaking his head at me. "How is it instructive to take babies' kazoos away? That's just mean."

"Good point. Grown-ups are mean and no fun. And nobody is telling me to grow up."

"Your landlord is telling you to grow up and the rock star machine that calls you a failure is telling you to grow up and the stack of bills in your mailbox is telling you to grow up and the show-offs are telling you to grow up and the *winners* are telling you to grow up—"

"Jesus, calm down. This is true. But it's all soooooo stupid."

He nods. "You don't listen."

"That's my secret." We're at the tents now, watching the bustle begin. "I play one chord. *One chord.* And it disappears, the stupid. Do you laugh at your own jokes?" He thinks about this, doesn't seem to know. "Well, you should. The funny ones, anyway."

❙ ❘ ❘ ▸ ▸ ▸

I play guitar in my shining white, shaky trailer and make notes in my script, which is now almost unreadable for all the pen marks: arrows and chordal notations, added paragraphs written over crossed-out ones. It's a million degrees hot in here. There is a stack of fan mail next to a vase of drying flowers and some gifts that were placed at the base of my mic stand after the shows: handmade jewelry and stickers, a child's drawing and a Polaroid of someone's dog with a word balloon drawn on the photo: "I am in a doghouse," referring to a song I wrote when I was fourteen. I don't like having that old song in my head, so that Polaroid makes me practice.

I *cannot* pay attention when I play guitar. In an unholy blend of passion and work, playing guitar is the part of me with a name racing to catch up with some weird dream entity that is continually making up new rules. *You think you can play this game, Kris? Think again.* One note is a purity; a line in a painting or a cell in a body, a foundational impulse upon which to grow something. Two notes then play against each other as intersecting lines or points vying for the same mark, allowing themselves to be shaped by friction and relativity. *You make your crummy little mark*, I think, *like shoes scuffing linoleum.* And three notes? Are a chord, of all things. In that, they are life-changing. Changed *my* life, anyway. What isn't there to learn from disparate elements shaping each other and creating a new impact together? How is that not love? Whether I should say that word out loud or *not*.

Because I'm synesthetic, chords have colors that splash all over each other. Add a few more notes and the melody inherent in every strike triggers reflection like a scent. The scent is actual molecules of a substance as a sound; as a vibrational accuracy returning you to a sense memory, telling some story you earned by living it. But not the you with a name, just the you with a body and the will to keep its atoms from flying apart. A song lies within that, impressing no one, yet leaving an impression. We make our mark on the linoleum, then slip our shoes off and walk away.

Staring down at my script, I'm struck by the difference between storytelling and lyrics. All words, all in English, all meant to be spoken by a mouth, to communicate; but conversational language moving events through a time frame – in other words, a story – is a learned form of clarity. It is taken in by an audience acting in the capacity of social creatures, and its effect lies in their willingness to adopt some of my sense memories as I relive a play-by-play. (Our differences would reject this alignment. Possibly because they don't like vomiting.) Their systems either take my ride or refuse to, in other words, as I choose to do in any conversation, any moment in another's presence.

A song is different, though. Another entity has entered the room then, and our shared impression of it has hit us in a different place. Not cerebral plus tactile but visceral: some big heart is made of all our hearts piled on top of each other, either relating and blending like these colors or defining our differences and highlighting those colors, making them more vibrant. That effect kicks in without any effort on our part. In fact, an effort to restrain or engage interferes with the process; that instantaneous absorption.

After forty years of songwriting, lyrics are still mysterious to me. Why do we speak in music? Poetry is real when it's real, of course, but there's an interesting counter-effect when we allow words to redefine themselves as percussive melody. If a musical piece is meant to incorporate voice—the instrument *voice*— it will sometimes ask your mouth to play along with pieces of conversation or stories it's heard, with dreams and memories and broken weather, with a twisted bastardization of language. We call it 'meaning,' groping for a term that describes the depth of visceral response to a song, but this kind of meaning communicates no ideas. Meaning redefines itself when we take cerebral off the table, thereby escaping the labeling-then-looking-away that we humans are so fond of; as if there's nothing else to be learned from this plane. It's touching to take Idea off the table in an industry whose only idea was: *sell*.

Shifting my hands high on the neck of the guitar to achieve a more ringing tone, I make a note in the script that this passage—a story about a fallen movie star—is to be read under a wistful twelfth fret hang. *How is that not manipulation?* I think. Bird calls can sound nostalgic, some frets sound more wistful. Just brushing up on the fundamentals, I guess. *Note to self: never forget that you sometimes suck.* And never forget that earth has all the shine we'll ever need, all laid out in front of every baby born to this place. The baby's fingerprints no less active than wrinkles earned over time, and vice versa. Take linear time out of the equation like that and we're speaking of a person's *essence* on both sides of the musician/listener equation.

Staring down at the lyrics in my script, I realize that they are the spine of this story and the weather around it. "Emotion" is a reductive term given the sweaty verbing here of some otherwise "normal" words one uses to communicate in conversational English. It's more like the muscle of experience spewed in images. This movie star's song is an underwater thing, with moments of cigar-chomping moguls' desks in Hollywood and a sweet melancholy minor-key fear through shaded palms. These images grow fists and lips capable of punching and kissing. I yell or whisper them until I fuck up and the lyrics grow dismal and un-alive. Crossing these out in the script, I also make a note in my song notebook to lose the third verse. *How 'bout lose every god-damn third verse?* Rescue everything from Boring. Who needs you to talk more than you already did?

The idea is: it's *not* you. The person writing and playing the song is a selfless selfhood of experience, hell bent on sharing . . . or even being ignored if that's best. An approximation of all the voices who might have carried a song across oceans or through fields, sung in bars or to children. The song *is*. Like the baby on earth, senses wrapped up and reflecting the stuff of here, tripping and falling. Glancing at the Polaroid that keeps shining a flashlight on my fourteen-year-old self and her attempt to find this language: no song is ever perfect, which drives us to write the next song.

All of this leads me to believe that what we're missing in the recording industry is exactly that: song as a language. We call music the universal language because we're born speaking it. We are so far from actual songs in the music business, from the *isness* of a song, that a dream, rarified and streamlined, is heard as strange. Unique as a fingerprint is an unmarketable concept and therefore these works are considered to be weeds. All things grow but only what serves "us" is valuable, so cut down anything that doesn't; it can't live if we want to thrive. If mankind is now an econ-omy, we will determine usefulness accordingly, and a recording industry—industrial production of sound copies—prefers to market by slimmer and slimmer margins of substance.

I gotta ask the comedian if he thinks we're weeds.

And by extension, so is everyone else. Anyone in a moment of clarity can write a true song. These moments are encouraged by humanity, discouraged by economy. My song notebook, I notice, is full of weeds. A whole garden of facilitating life which serves no economic function. A cooperation, not a competition. The essence of songwriting's future.

A gentle knock on my open trailer door and I turn around to see the comedian standing on the silver metal steps in the fading sun. "Can I come in?"

"You can't come into my trailer," I tell him.

"Why not?"

"I dunno . . ." I close my notebook so he can't read my lyrics. "Just seems wrong." He waits, leans in the door frame. Pushing a tub full of beer and soda cans into the corner, I point at an avocado-colored miniature couch. "You could sit there, if you want. Do you think we're weeds?"

"Of course we're weeds. Anyone who doesn't serve Power is a weed, always has been." He sits down on the couch, looks at me blankly. "I thought you might have beer."

"I do have beer. It's warm and it's been warm for weeks. Want it?"

He picks up a can and studies it. "I uh . . . bet there's ice somewhere in Australia."

"There was ice in Australia a few weeks ago," I nod. "In there." I point at the plastic tub. "Back when the beer was cold. So Power is money now?"

Opening the beer, he sighs over it. "I'd like to talk to my friend about this movie I saw one boiling hot Christmas," he says. "*It's a Wonderful Life* with Jimmy Stewart and . . . Jimmy Stewart and . . ." He takes a sip of his beer and thinks.

"Donna Reed."

". . . and Donna Reed. And some shit about sunflowers and love."

I stick both my thumbs up at him. "Sounds good, buddy. Fun fact: Donna Reed had her own TV show? And once, Dennis the Menace visited her at her TV show house. Was standing on her front porch when she answered the door. And Donna said, 'Dennis!' as if television was a town, where they all lived inside the little boxes in our houses and could potentially know each other, or at least know each other's names and ring their doorbells." He stares, taking another sip of his hot beer. "Blew my mind," I add.

Looking up at the trailer ceiling, he pictures this. "That *is* kind of mind-blowing. And I imagine you're telling me the Jack of Diamonds gets left out of that poker game?"

"Not much of a stretch, right? The entertainment industry sells us a facsimile of life which we adopt, blurring our senses, coming between us and our 'low status' experience. Private things are uncelebrated things."

"A big party you aren't invited to," he agrees, squinting to read the dog's word balloon on the Polaroid stuck to my mirror. "This beer is very warm."

"It's *hot*. Hot beer."

"Can I go yet?"

I throw my hands up, rolling my eyes. "I didn't want you here at *all*. It's *wrong*."

Standing up, he walks slowly down the rickety metal stairs, shaking my whole trailer with each step.

"Maybe *It's a Wonderful Life* just means that life is wonderful," I call down to him. "Who knows?" He doesn't turn around, just stops at the bottom of the stairs. "Don't overthink it, you know? Nobody shines more than anyone else. Real life is real music is real anything. Even that thing *you* do."

He talks over his shoulder. "Comedy."

"Right. And we look away from Television Town when it gets boring, to feel things with our own fingertips again." He turns around, trying to wear his most patient expression. "When they try to sell us *names* as vessels of genius, they take quality away from our bodies, when we know better. Genius is not in a person with a name, but in everyone's inspired moments."

"Can I go yet?" he asks.

"No. The audience needs to make their *own* lives, their *own* art. We just hint at that, calling ourselves 'artists' and co-opting them for profit."

"They're all geniuses," he states flatly.

"Yeah! Well . . . there is genius. Inspired moments happen, always have, in every life, right? *That's* genius. Let's get back to *everyone* feeling their stories as they play out. There'd be so much laughing, so many songs, that you and I could actually work . . . just enough to pass the hat, because we'd all speak that universal language again."

He pauses, raising his eyebrows, as his patient look slips, then walks away, holding up his beer in salute. "God help us!" he calls.

꜒ ꜒ ꜒ ꜒ ꜒ ꜒

Nobody vomits at my show, which I consider to be a win. Slipping out the back of the tent during the last applause, I see my comedian already there, studying the night sky, so I join him in the Quaker meeting part of our evening. When we only talk if we have something to say.

Bats rustle, some fly away from their trees in skittery formation. It's dark back here, all lights trained on people leaving the fairgrounds. The big rabbit peeks his head around the edge of my tent. "What're you two up to?" he whispers.

We look at him. "Just avoiding people," I answer. "Hey, we have a gun for you. And a kite."

"Oh my god, really?" He looks genuinely touched. "What kind of gun?"

"Water. The fun kind. From a bone museum."

"A fun gun!" squeals the rabbit, balancing on his platform sandals. "Next time you go to a museum, give me a call, okay? I'd like to do some touristy stuff before I leave. The more cultured, the better!" Someone on the other side of the tent calls the rabbit and he waves, taking off.

"I'll bring you your prizes!" I call after him, then pat my friend on the arm. "The word 'cultured'—" I begin.

"Here we go . . ." He rolls his eyes, then closes them to keep me out of his head.

"—implies that we'd like to keep up with the quality we all agree is shining in our culture. I *like* that. I just don't like to see that impulse manipulated."

He sits in silence, eyes still shut. Seems to be falling asleep. "Is that a question?"

"I'm open to your comments. Take your time. The bats are just waking up."

Now his eyes are open, but barely. "The bats are the best." A sky obscured with leathery wings. "I imagine we play a social role in whatever populace we find ourselves born into," he murmurs.

I sit up straight. "We're gonna fly kites tonight, you know? Approximate the flying foxes' flying. That's all I mean."

"Yeah. I have this image of the three of us on yonder hill, flying midnight kites."

"Right. We just keep trying stuff." Noises from inside our tents. It's time to pack up and go. "Midnight kites with a giant rabbit could be a cool thing that rises to the top of our impression of culture, no matter how small or brief that *genius* is. That inspired moment." He's actually snoring now. Drunk on hot beer maybe, so I figure he doesn't hear this: "Here's a thing: I'm not sure monetizing laughter and musical response is even okay. I don't know that we should *ask* that our rent be paid." Guess I'm talking to myself. We aren't flying kites tonight.

I try to leave quietly, but lifting the tent flap to retrieve my guitar startles him.

"Give my love to *It's a Wonderful Life.*"

Staring down at him. "Sleep in your trailer."

"And leave these stars?" He spreads his arms to the sky. "Goodnight, Ms. K." He doesn't know I fly out in the morning, that my run is over. *Better this way. Goodnight is always better than goodbye.*

"Little boys balancing on fountains," I remind him, walking away with my guitar.

"And blue octopuses," he adds. "Purvey that venom, sister!"

A Loveliness

Reflections of ladybugs crawling up windows make their way across a yellow Formica table in a New Orleans kitchen. "They've been walking for days," Cheech says. "I guess they're all on the roof now?"

I watch the insect shadows on my hands: little gray circles moving through streaks of rain. The circles march along my fingers and then down the table. It's good to be back home in New Orleans, but I left unanswered questions in Australia. Left a sad comedian in Australia. I know we were beating each other over the head with the Jack of Diamonds, but we were so close to solving our equations of lostness and foundness. Think of the *songs* that could happen if we could make that raw math work. It'd be amazing.

I had finished my festival work in a daze, then flown back to New Orleans and her richness; her suffering and violence and partying ease; her redemption through sin and whatever gets you through the long, long night. The woman I'm with is a Blackfoot acupuncturist who tends to read people's minds without knowing it. She puts two cups of tea down and joins me at her kitchen table, placing her hand alongside mine in the ladybug shadows to watch them make their watery way down her fingers. "Guess what a swarm of ladybugs is called," she says. "I looked it up: it's called a loveliness."

"Whaaaaaaaaaaaaat." I blink. "There's no way that's possible. And if it is? It's the only thing that matters."

She nods. "I know, right?"

"When kids learn to speak, this is the first thing they need to know." I shake my head.

"And we just found out." Cheech blows on her tea. "Drink your tea, it's good for you."

The tea smells like basement. Taking a careful sip, I learn that it tastes like basement, too. "Tastes like basement."

She nods and takes a sip of hers. "How was Australia?"

"Hot. Hot Christmas. Cool bats. I told some gross stories. Felt bad about it."

"Don't carry it." She shrugs and points at my cup. "That's why I gave you this tea. You have some toxic stories in your liver."

"I do? Story poison?" I ask. She doesn't seem to feel sorry for me; she never does. "And all I gotta do to get clean is drink basement?"

"Basement will release the poison into your system. It's up to you what you do with it after that." More ladybugs appear in her window, gliding slowly *up*. "Transmutation is a thing."

"Feel poison. Doesn't sound fun. Or fair."

"It's not fun," she says flatly, "and nothing is fair. So it isn't *un*fair."

I try the tea again, but basement tastes *so* much like basement. There is a gross story in my goddamn teacup; how's *that* gonna help? "Right . . . is there something *else* I can do to get clean?"

Cheech studies me, then grabs my arm to feel my pulse. "I'll stick some needles in you, if you like."

A scratching, scrambling noise as her dog stumbles into the kitchen and barrels into the wall. We watch him recover, shaking his head. "He okay?" I ask her.

"Yeah, he's just sliding around in his sock feet cuz he's bored. What poison stories did you tell in Australia?"

"It wasn't Australia's fault, it was a sad man and the poison *questions* we asked. Being across the world, in another hemisphere, is a nice opportunity to review."

She nods, petting her dog as he stretches and smiles. He doesn't seem any worse off for having smashed his head into a wall. "You want Now to change. Not a good mindset."

"I want the *future* to change." The Jack of Diamonds, Donna Reed, dinosaur bones, bats and water pistols; my drunk buddy's clarity and confusion. "There was a big rabbit and a little blue octopus." Cheech raises her eyebrows. "Big bats called flying foxes and it was nice to be lost. I had a black and white movie on repeat for a month and I lived in a black and white building, but there was crazy color everywhere else. Summer in winter, you know?" Her eyebrows are still up, waiting. "The sad man and I were asking each other how we'd gotten there. To the point of straddling these Big Bangs of purpose—songs and laughing—and trying to attract attention. One impulse seems so right and the other feels so wrong. But the only way to work as a songwriter is to attract attention. Same with him." I picture him the last way I saw him: arms folded, folded up in a folding chair. I want him to unfold. "He tries to make people laugh, of all things."

"That's nice." She seems to mean this, but she's very wrong. What my friend does is not nice at *all*.

"I guess. Nicer than what *I* do. I make them vomit."

"I do, too, sometimes," she says thoughtfully. "Medicine can be a tough sell." She looks down into her teacup full of basement.

Medicine! "Is medicine a similar discipline?" I ask her. This has never occurred to me, though I probably put songs in the category of the healing arts. I speak slowly because I'm thinking out loud. "Is there an inspired moment that moves you to create a new body of work? An effect that is then other than you?"

Cheech is still looking into her cup of basement. She speaks to it. "I facilitate, yes. The energetic is between the cure and the patient and I facilitate that exchange. The patient cures itself."

My eyes must be huge. "Holy shit, that's *it*." This was the missing piece. My comedian and I were trying to articulate our role in this exchange—to solve for x—without realizing that the equation itself has very little to do with us. The Jack of Diamonds is a *messenger* and that's all he should ever be. All *we* should ever be. "So . . . you and me and anyone like us, facilitates an exchange?" I say to Cheech. "We are only necessary in as much as we bring the medicine to the person who needs it. *We* are not the story and the more we try to control that exchange, the more we try to *make* ourselves the story, the less effective the medicine. When they try to ascribe an inflated importance to the middleman, you get stars and greed and there is no longer any medicine at all."

Cheech nods. "In my field, they call that a God complex."

"They should call it that in *my* field, too, because that's what they think they are. Bigger than mortals." Solving for x is then a blurring of its import. A messenger straddles, ghostlike and evidencing an uncertainty principle. We shouldn't play to external valuations or we'll be behind the game and unable to help *any*one. Never play to the market; remain a response, drop your weapons, your self-concept. Real songs will wait in the ether for us to achieve this. The future is filled not just with heartbeats looking to race, but with organisms looking to shrink and expand.

In other words, if there *is* a future for songwriting, the stars will be the songs themselves.

Cheech sounds like she's discussing office supplies. Nothing ever excites her. "A shaman endures not just physical pain but social shame," she tells me. "Humility. The opposite of a God complex."

"And could anyone—I mean everyone—in an inspired moment, facilitate that exchange?"

"Yeah, well," she laughs. "Prob'ly why I can't afford new tires."

"That's kinda what we were talking about. My fear when it comes to professional songwriters is the same one we all have about politicians: most people who want that job aren't cut out for it. They're in it for status and if you believe in somebodies and nobodies, songs won't come to you. But I think just about anybody who isn't trying to attract attention *could* write songs. At least sometimes."

Her dog slobbers on her hand and flops down to the floor, sighing. Wiping the drool off on her skirt, she tells him he's a good boy and then asks him if he's a good boy. Then says that he is again. "Yeah. Wanting fame and money'd be the first indicator that somebody's missed the point entirely, no matter how they're trying to get it."

"I wouldn't let a show-off write *my* soundtrack." I try basement tea again. Maybe the bitterness'll clear me of my own bitterness. "Not much medicine in the music business."

"Well *duh-uh*," she shakes her head. "Look at Western medicine: it's a business, too. A business that fights symptoms, of all things; when symptoms are

how a body fights disease. These are suicidal ventures."
The chickens outside murmur and scrabble.

"I got fifty bucks in my truck," I tell her. "Want
it?"

"That's not how it works, Kris."

"That's *exactly* how it works. Toward some new
tires." I grab my wallet to see how much is in it.

Cheech smirks. "I've seen *your* truck's tires."

"My tires just suck because I'm a lousy *person*," I
explain. "A bad truck mom."

Selfie culture where people are ads for themselves,
under the sun of Narcissus: if this is the future,
we need to bring back the past. How do you find
people who might need the medicine you carry? The
Polaroid you took of a song and carried across the
world or next door. How do you participate without
becoming part of the problem? I reach down to pet
the slobbery dog under the table, who pants up at
me with a smile that makes me smile back.

"Culture is in lives," Cheech says, reading my
mind like she always does. "Think small world, big
picture." Scooping up both cups of tea, she empties
them into the sink, then soaps up a sponge. "Every
culture is in quiet lives."

"Oh, that's beautiful," I hum at the dog, who
drops his head back onto his paws. Cheech grabs

a dishtowel covered in dark smudges and dries our cups with it. "So," I say to the dog under the table, "comedy, music and medicine. Laughing takes down ego before it does damage, music takes down melodrama before it obscures drama, and medicine balances us when contagion and symptomatic response endanger our systems."

The palm trees in her yard brush against the window. We listen to the brushing together. "They all balance us," Cheech points out. All of these disciplines, when evolved, are an un-damaging. "So they're all a kind of medicine."

"That's interesting, cuz my friend called it venom. Said we were purveyors of venom."

"Maybe *you* are," she says thoughtfully.

"Just one concern," I tell her. "That the only way to monetize within a broken system is to participate in a disease. We don't treat cancer by encouraging inflammatory growth of those 'successful' mutations, right?"

She looks at me, blank. "Successful mutations."

"I mean that culturally, we reward the most dangerous aspects of personality: narcissism, exhibitionism, selfishness. The culture's cancer."

Drying her hands on the grimy dishtowel. "No, no, no, no, no . . . *we* don't. Look away from pretend power."

I nod. "Okay, right. Healthy cells work *for* the system." I know what to tell my comedian buddy now about the Jack of Diamonds and his physical and metaphysical path. Glancing up at the window, dazzled by the loveliness of ladybugs again, my speech slows; they're so hypnotizing. "We sell medicine, so only *some* people should take it; it's not for everyone. Don't expand your audience, refine it." She nods, still smirking at me like she always does. "Where do you wanna put needles in me?"

"God, all over." She shakes her head. "You're a mess."

I grimace at her. "I mean where in your *house*?"

"Oh. Hmmm." She stands in her kitchen doorway, peering into the living room. "Let's find you a place with a nice view of the ladybugs."

♩ ♪ ♪ ♪ ♪ ♪

Spontaneity as synchronicity: the music wants to happen, songs feel like lightning. We beat the surface of water, shape trees to make instruments, we hit cardboard boxes in basements, sing wildly, politely, together and alone. We build instruments no one has ever heard before and we build instruments people have built for thousands of years, then play them like no one has ever heard before. We find broken ones and bring them back to life. People make music for joy and anguish, for parties and lullabies, for community and solitude.

We're born with an unselfconscious response to music and the ability to inspire that in others. A true song proves its worth as a life form, as a successful organism, or it doesn't cross oceans or the blood–brain barrier; doesn't embed itself in a child's memory banks. And we are all children when it comes to our memory banks.

The recording industry's business model was based on copies; a model which only worked for a short time. Promotional money processed product with inflammatory power: the bought spotlight. A healthy song, a selfless endeavor, a participation, a gift . . . will not earn the money-backed spotlight, as it has a beating heart and unique fingerprint, which we no longer equate with value if we equate value with money. But the beating heart? The fingerprint, the impulse to breathe that is real music? Doesn't value money and it cannot lose. This is *musical* success, not music *business* success. It is infinite and unstoppable, like a loveliness of ladybugs. This Big Bang in a quiet American kitchen is culture, not economy.

The ladybugs continue to slide up my friend's windows, which is hypnotic and slightly disturbing.

"You think they know what they're doing?" I call into the kitchen, trying not to shift any of the needles sticking out of my arms and legs. Cheech pressed me into a chair near the ladybugs to try and clean me of poison stories, but now I begin to wish I had another viewing option. Something about the inexorability of their climb is off-putting.

"Who?"

"Your ladybugs! Or did we mess up the little plates in their heads with pollution or microwaves or something?"

Appearing in the doorway, she watches the ones in front of me I can't seem to look away from. "I hear ya. I don't know. It's been a few days now." We watch a streak of water take a few ladybugs down the glass as it drips into the frame. "Check out *this* one," she says, moving toward the window. Pointing at a ladybug crawling down the glass, she follows it with her finger. "It's going back for the others."

"It *is?*"

"I think so. Watch this. It's turning around and leading these up to the roof." I squint at the glass, but all I see is a buncha bugs. "Are ladybugs like bees? Do they play different roles in their society?"

"I wish I knew." Her bug is definitely turning around now and there are bugs behind it, but I dunno. We watch the ladybugs together. More streaks of warm rain catch some and they slip back down the glass. "When I treat patients," she says thoughtfully, "I find a pulse in their system which leads me to the problem. Then I lead them to the solution, but both are in their bodies."

Studying a needle sticking out of my calf muscle, which is wrapped around the two jagged shin bones that made Australians vomit, she twists the silver thread of metal and an electric burn spreads up my leg. I grit my teeth at the strangeness. Noticing my discomfort, she does it again, then sits back on her ottoman, and focuses on the window again, a sunbreak bathing her face in rainbow through the water droplets.

Maybe there really *are* ladybugs who back up and lead the others up the glass. Maybe they're helping us quietly. Maybe all the unheard music is resonant energy shooting up into what matters, into us. Songs are still in the human sphere, where they have always been: wild voices telling wild stories. Attention is a misapprehension of life living itself. We only live hard and strong when we're unmeasured, uncelebrated, unselfconscious.

⅃ ⅂ ▸ ▸ ▸ ▸

It isn't easy to extricate my bike from Cheech's overgrown backyard. Lots of vines and chickens and rusty beer cans full of seedlings. Pulling wildflowers out of my spokes, I realize I feel closer to knowing that music has a substantive future. Say we bring Life back to life: reintroduce a healthy biology to every sphere, every endeavor, each moment. Neither lofty nor base, neither snob appeal nor bandwagon appeal. Bring nature to the denatured, because anything else is an aberration; a misguided attempt to achieve by defeating others.

Music would then be reflective of a state like animal or child, with nothing to gain but existence itself. No winning, no 'big.' Not big money or big names. Not self-expression, but *selfless* expression, using our unique fingerprints to offer ... what? What the hell *is* music? Maybe we can't know that. Our response is akin to laughter, to tears, to fight and flight, to symptomatic response, to lightning strike or sleep, to falling in love and staying in love.

I knock over, like, six beer cans full of seedlings, trying to wrestle flowers out of my bike tires, so I have to bend down to push all the dirt back into place, and when I do, I see that they're all little sunflowers. *Oh nifty! Like our kindergarten paper cups. Except beer cans.* Cheech opens the window above me to stare down, looking bored. "Stop. It's fine."

I squint up at her. "No, it's not. I broke your baby flowers." I shove more dirt into a beer can and try to get a sunflower seedling to stand upright.

"I'll take care of it, dork. Just do me a favor and tell me what my ladybugs are doing."

Righting the beer can and steadying it, I stand up and try to pick out the ladybug parade from siding, hurricane shutters and shingles. Just looks like a few bugs on a few panes of glass. "Well," I tell her. "It's less dramatic from out here."

"It is? Shoot."

I twist my mouth up in sympathy. "Were you thinking horror movie?"

Cheech stretches her neck out the window as far as it goes, then twists her head around. "Either that or something magic."

"Dude, you *are* magic," I tell her. "You don't need *more* magic."

She thinks about this, studying the chipped paint. "Let's try to assume that there's always more magic," she says.

We Duel at Dawn

My comedian stands on a beach in southern California, facing the ocean. He has dressed up for me in his goofiest Hawaiian trunks, green sunglasses and a T-shirt with the Equal Rights Amendment on it. He's holding a lit cigarette in his left hand and a trucker cap in his right. In the back pockets of his bathing suit, sticking out at crazy angles, are our two kites from Sydney; our dinosaur water guns are precariously balanced in a holster he wears loose around his hips. He looks genuinely nuts, but he looks genuinely nuts for *me* and for that, I'm grateful. Didn't ask for it, but still.

It's cold and sunny, the beach empty except for a guy and his dog, who both look like Nixon. Pulling a playing card out of his pocket, my friend attempts to shove it into the bill of his trucker cap, but it blows away. So he puts the cigarette in his mouth and chases it across the sand. I frown. "I thought you quit smoking."

"I did," he says, wading in to catch the playing card as it flutters into the water. "Like eight times."

I watch him blow sand off the card. "Cuz you're tense."

"It's *all* cuz I'm tense. Everything is cuz I'm tense." He presses the card into his hat and looks at me, the Jack of Diamonds on his forehead staring after Nixon and Dog Nixon.

"Awwwww . . . lookin' good!" I tell him and he nods, which makes the card blow away again.

"Whoopsie," he mutters, chasing it back into the water.

I watch him fumble with it in the ripples. "How'd you get it to stick to your hat?" Catching it again, he holds it up and shows me a fat piece of tape on the back—wet and covered with sand—then slaps his forehead with the card and he's wearing it on his face. "It's very cool that you thought to bring our talisman."

"Jack o' Diamonds?" he asks through the cigarette. "He's more like a mascot."

"Yeah. Both good luck." The ocean is an odd slate color. It's the kind of day when you can smell the salt in it. "I went to a witch doctor in the Bywater in New Orleans? And she says he's a messenger."

"Witch doctor."

"Uh huh," I nod. "Wanna walk?"

He takes a plastic dinosaur head out of its holster. "Yes ma'am. Gonna reload first."

I watch him carefully fill the yellow water gun in tiny waves, replace it, then fill the red one. Guess he gave the blue one to the rabbit after I left Australia. "I'm sorry I didn't say goodbye," I tell him. He says nothing, just tries to angle the hole on top of the red dinosaur's head in the water. "I thought 'goodnight' was better. If that's not true, I'm sorry."

Carefully replacing the plastic cap on the squirt gun, he stands up and holds it out to me. "Goodnight was better."

I check his face to make sure he's telling the truth, but there isn't much left of his head what with the hat and the Jack, the sunglasses and cigarette. He's also unshaven. "Witch doctor's my friend. Really, I should call her a medicine woman cuz she *is* one. She had ladybugs all over her roof. Swarms of them. And guess what a swarm of ladybugs is called."

"A murder."

"That's crows."

"A gang."

I grab his arm in enthusiasm. "A *loveliness!*"

His jaw drops. "That's not true."

"It totally is. A loveliness. Anyway. I wanted to know what she thought about the Jack of Diamonds."

Looking down at me sadly, he says, "Do we have a future?"

"I don't know. My concern is songwriting, really. But I like talking to you about you cuz you're such a case."

"Oh thank you." He clears his throat. "Thank you very much."

We stop to watch a couple kids run with a surfboard from the parking lot to the water, clamber onto the board and then kick into the breakers. "You help me see aesthetic response more clearly because laughing at ego is so genuine, so spontaneous and so human." The younger kid tries to stand on the board while the other gently props him up. "Musical response seems more mysterious, but I imagine you gotta be genuine, spontaneous and human to get real music. Also, you're all fucked up about selling."

He blows more smoke into the wind, which the wind blows right back at him. "Would you like to submit something?"

"If I may." The wind picks up and we turn away from the kids in the ocean, start walking slowly again, and I speak slowly as well, so I can think clearly. "I think all truly inspired moments are songs. I was born to think this. Others have different templates. But musical response would be the potential resonance of these moments. It's biology plus love.

"So no such thing as a stupid song. If it's stupid, it's not a song, just a selfishness. If it's real, you can't call it stupid. Look what marketing did to sex, which is another biology plus love." A beat while we reflect on this sadness. "The symptomatic response that my New Orleans lady facilitates in her patients? Is what we encourage in others by reinvigorating an inspired moment. Biology plus love. We are alive, we are a social species, this is a social endeavor."

He twitches. "You and I aren't social."

"Right. Uh . . . our introversion serves our initial focus."

"Gotcha."

"And don't interrupt." I make my best brain-buzzing face at him. "Songs and medicine and laughing at ego cannot be reduced to a commercial facsimile. Commercial music is a commercial, not music; not biology plus love." He opens his mouth to speak again, so I interrupt him as fast as I can. "We? Are messengers, like the Jack of Diamonds. We are not purveyors of venom, but of medicine intended only for the few who need it to balance. We are not the message, we didn't write the message, and it's not for *us*."

We walk in silence. The Nixon-dog we saw earlier races past, followed by his Nixon-owner, who's stumbling down the sand with a kind of jogging/chasing motion. My comedian doesn't say anything. "Period." I splay my hands at him. "You can interrupt now."

"That's *it*? How are we gonna survive?"

Punching him in the arm. "We're not!" I announce happily.

"God, you punch me a lot."

"Not necessarily, anyway. But music will and laughing will and that's the medicine here. Cheech can't even afford truck tires and she's freakin' *magic*. But when people get bad-broken instead of good-broken, we can help. We're leaving the century of product. We're lucky to witness this."

"Kris," he shakes his head.

"Alright, alright. But you know how it feels when inspiration wakes you up. Live there. Share it."

"From the sidewalk," he moans, "where I'm gonna live." Mashing his hands into his hat, he crumples the playing card.

"Or from your goddamn *mansion* if somebody gives you money," I fuss at him, "but it doesn't matter. You have a body, use it for love and work."

Unmashing his trucker cap and turning it backwards on his head, he hands me the Jack of Diamonds. "Present," he grumbles, taking a last drag of his cigarette, which he carefully puts out on the sole of his sneaker and shoves into his pocket. He's *good*. He won't litter. He won't fill the world with garbage.

"It's not true or just to be a king or a queen or a leading man or lady." I have become earnest, can't help it. "We're character actors because the truth is that we're *all* character actors. We're unique like everyone. We're Nature, we're not against her."

I wait, watching the reflection of waves in his sunglasses where his eyes should be, but he says nothing else. Putting his big hands on my small shoulders, he just stares. The question of survival hangs between us, always. "When the work carries a true moment to others. *That* is our survival. That is a song. That was the past and that is the future." I look up at him. "So we call no attention to ourselves, but we're willing to walk our talk with our bodies. We show *up*, we don't show off." He says nothing. "Industries are our Goliath and they will fall. They'll fall *winning* but we don't have to play that game."

"The only game in town," he reminds me. "The future can't be the past."

Wincing, I study the foamy water. "Take linear time off our poker table," I tell him. "Is it dawn yet?" I ask him. "Can we duel now?"

"When *aren't* we dueling?" And he softens. "Yeah, twenty paces." He holds up his yellow squirt gun, peering through the plastic sight. The surfboard kids catch a gentle wave, riding it all the way in to the sand. "I will try to be on your side."

"It's not *my* side," I shrug.

Adjusting his trucker cap, he drops his shoulders and takes a deep breath, then pauses. "I don't think our dinosaurs can shoot from twenty paces away," he points out.

I look up at him. "When do we fly the kites?"

"After we duel." He considers this. "Well . . . the survivor can fly *both* kites."

"At this moment," I intone, "we are neither murderer nor victim."

He shivers happily. "We are not. Yet. Blue."

"Ten paces," I tell him, shoving the Jack of Diamonds in my pocket. "You're gonna be so damn wet with a small amount of sea water and you'll never see it coming. We're dueling for the future." He nods and we turn away from each other, standing back-to-back with our plastic dinosaurs at the ready. We have past and future, we have ourselves and each other; we have today, and we have nothing. The small surfboard kid slips and the older boy grabs his arm, steadies him.

About the Series

Each volume in the FUTURES Series presents a vision imagined by an accomplished writer and subject expert. The series seeks to publish a diverse range of voices, covering as wide-ranging a view as possible of our potential prospects. Inspired by the brilliant 'To-Day and To-Morrow' books from a century ago, we ask our authors to write in a spirit of pragmatic hope, and with a commitment to map out potential future landscapes, highlighting both beauties and dangers. We hope the books in the FUTURES Series will inspire readers to imagine what might lie ahead, to figure out how they might like the future to look, and, indeed, to think about how we might get there

Professor Max Saunders and Dr Lisa Gee
Series originators, University of Birmingham

The FUTURES Series was originally conceived by Professor Max Saunders and Dr Lisa Gee, both of whom work at the University of Birmingham. Saunders is Interdisciplinary Professor of Modern Literature and Culture and the author of *Imagined Futures: Writing, Science, and Modernity in the To-Day and To-Morrow* book series, 1923-31 (OUP 2019), and Gee is Assistant Professor in Creative Writing and Digital Media and Research Fellow in Future Thinking.

To find out more about their Future Thinking work visit www.birmingham.ac.uk/futures